ETHICS OF
THE WORD

VOICES IN THE
CATHOLIC CHURCH TODAY

JAMES F. KEENAN, SJ

A SHEED & WARD BOOK

ROWMAN & LITTLEFIELD PUBLISHERS, INC.
Lanham · Boulder · New York · Toronto · Plymouth, UK

A SHEED & WARD BOOK

Published by Rowman & Littlefield Publishers, Inc.
A wholly owned subsidiary of The Rowman & Littlefield Publishing Group, Inc.
4501 Forbes Boulevard, Suite 200, Lanham, Maryland 20706
http://www.rowmanlittlefield.com

Estover Road, Plymouth PL6 7PY, United Kingdom

British Library Cataloguing in Publication Information Available

Library of Congress Cataloging-in-Publication Data
Keenan, James F.
  Ethics of the word : voices in the Catholic Church today / James F. Keenan.
    p. cm.
  Includes index.
  ISBN 978-0-7425-9956-7 (cloth : alk. paper) — ISBN 978-0-7425-9957-4 (pbk. : alk.
paper) — ISBN 978-0-7425-9958-1 (electronic)
  1. Communication—Religious aspects—Catholic Church. 2. Communication—Moral
and ethical aspects. 3. Christian ethics—Catholic authors. I. Title.
  BX1795.C67K44 2010
  241'.672—dc22   2009050216

∞™ The paper used in this publication meets the minimum requirements of American
National Standard for Information Sciences—Permanence of Paper for Printed Library
Materials, ANSI/NISO Z39.48-1992.

Printed in the United States of America

For Maura

CONTENTS

Part II: The Humanity of Our Discourse

Part III: Forms of Christian Discourse

Contents

ACKNOWLEDGMENTS

I want to acknowledge my students, particularly the undergraduates who gambled and took my course at Boston College on Church Leadership Ethics in the Spring 2004. This was my first undergraduate course in thirteen years! These students simply alerted me to the fact that language and words are central to the life of the church; if we compromise our words, we compromise ourselves.

I also want to thank the staff at *Church* magazine where I have been a contributor to the morals column for the past twenty years. Many of the essays in this collection originally appeared in that column. I have since redone each of these essays and added newer ones to this collection. Over the years the editor, Liz O'Connor, and her staff have been superb in helping me to develop my arguments. She and her colleagues at *Church* have been simply wonderful to work with.

Finally, I have been blessed with wonderful family and friends. I want to single out one of them, Maura Early. Years ago, when my niece Megan was combating cancer at Children's Hospital, I needed to rely on many people. But one stood out: if I ever called her or asked her to do anything, it would be done—from picking up family members to staying with Megan. Maura was always there. To her, I dedicate this book for her friendship and fidelity: her word has always been true.

Introduction

As I See and Hear It

In the early years of this past decade, as a priest and a Catholic theological ethicist living in Boston, I became involved in commenting on what we now refer to as the sexual abuse crisis. It was a very painful period in the life of the church, listening to the struggles of the victims and the confusion of the laity, while priests and bishops remained somewhat silent. Their silence, coupled with the charges and accusations, made for an unfortunate context, and not until Archbishop Sean O'Malley came to Boston in 2003 did we begin to see an end to the crisis in sight.

I wanted, however, to make a contribution in light of the crisis toward greater unity and integrity in the church. I found that a major challenge for the future was learning to communicate better with one another in the church. With so much negativity around, I wanted to offer a positive way of moving forward. Moreover, there was something deeply religious about discussing how we should reflect on what we say and how we speak to one another. After all, the Gospel of John witnesses to the fact that in the beginning was the Word and the Word was with God and the Word was God.

This collection begins, then, with some of my own reflections on the crisis. During that time what most struck me as signs of hope were the dialogues that emerged in light of the crisis: the "Report on the Crisis in the Catholic Church" seemed to be one of the first fruits of hope, coming from a fairly cohesive group of lay leaders discussing pathways for the future of the church. By engaging one another, not by speaking alone, they were commissioned to help the episcopacy specifically and the church generally to imagine itself after the crisis.

The Voice of the Faithful was another strong innovation, one that originated by no more than the exercise in a parish where people could meet to talk. In its earliest days, the members of Voice of the Faithful became overridingly committed to the vision that the church's well-being would be restored by letting its members search together for the truth through dialogue. Similarly, universities responded by hosting conferences and initiatives in which the search for reform would be positive, traditionally rooted, and of practical significance.

Because of these developments, I begin this work with two very different topics related to the crisis: first, the initiatives that promoted integral discussion as essential to the future of the church and then, classes with undergraduate and graduate students who eventually began to express their views in light of the crisis.

I do not see, however, my interest in dialogue limited to or singularly dependent on the crisis. Undeniably, in light of the crisis, as a church we began to think differently, as lay people started speaking more and more their minds in public, as bishops sought to provide leadership, and as some priests and theologians became prophetic in reading the signs of the times.

I began to think that I could do a series of essays on an Ethics of the Word, as I called this vision that I was trying to articulate. Could there be a way of reflecting how words actually shape and promote community, unity, and integrity? Could I consider the ways of language? Could I reflect on those ways to see how they could fortify the ordinary life of the church?

As I began working out my ideas, I left the crisis as a context of reflection. I wanted something less immediate and more enduring about the life of the church, and so I went to a variety of contexts: from the destruction by Katrina to the sudden death of my mom, I began to think about how we talk and why that matters. I wanted to speak about lying and promise-keeping, about civil discourse and truth-telling to hurt people, about beautiful words and challenging ones, about the human voice and apologies. I wanted to cover a variety of topics, all and each related to the way we talk.

I published many of the original thoughts for these essays in *Church* magazine. In this collection I expanded the ideas and visited anew each of the many topics I originally proposed. But I found myself moving from one topic to another with a surprising realization that there were many more issues related to the Ethics of the Word than I had thought.

In this collection, then, I try to give the essays a certain directionality. After considering what an Ethics of the Word would look like, I treat four basic themes in each successive part. First, under the "humanity of our discourse," I discuss the human components to discourse: voice, conscience, memory, desires, etc. Second, I examine actual forms of discourse: teaching, conversations, civil discourse, vocational experiences, and apologizing, among others. This section looks at the many ways we interact with one another verbally.

Third, I was struck by words. How are we affected by words? We just heard a congressman shout out at the president of the United States, "You lie." These are only two words, but together they become a stunningly powerful accusation in a very specific context. What about more benevolent words, like *friend, home, love, thank you*? A word can capture and express so much. Do we appreciate this? Thus, I dedicate five chapters about words that help us understand greetings and farewells and life and death. Finally, as Christians we all know the theological virtues of faith, hope, and charity, but what do they look like when we start talking about them?

Still these essays, like this work, are not meant to be comprehensive. On the contrary, since I think that this is the very first work of its kind, this collection is meant to prompt the reader to see that the Word in Christian life must guide us to more responsible ways of building up the church. They are meant to stimulate new ideas, open new discussions, and promote within the church a sustained way of speaking that is rich, respectful, and honest, a model to the world that we try to serve. Finally, they are to generate other topics, revisit major themes, and challenge the reader to name other issues about the Word that need to be addressed.

I hope you find here a collection of essays for your life and the life of the church and that through these essays we come to appreciate anew why it is that what we say and how we say it often has tremendous effect on one another.

Part I

A CHURCH IN NEED OF NEW WAYS OF LIVING THE TRUTH IN LOVE

Chapter One

ETHICS INSIDE THE CHURCH: LOOKING BACK, LOOKING FORWARD

At the end of February 2004, the ten lay members of the National Review Board for the Protection of Children and Young People released their "Report on the Crisis in the Catholic Church in the United States." The 145-page report was undoubtedly a keystone in developing the foundations for a more reconciled church in the future: it was designed to assist those involved in this work, most notably the bishops' conference, lay movements, priests' associations, and organizations of victims/survivors of abuse. The careful report prompts us to look back at what happened in the crisis precipitated by clergy who abused minors and by bishops who ignored the calls to protect children. In its recommendations, it also prompts us to look forward, considering what needs to happen in the weeks, months, and years ahead.

This dynamic of both looking back to understand and looking forward to reform has been put to good use with ever greater frequency over the past five years. Looking back has been and remains an important exercise. Were it not for the victims/survivors who have repeatedly called the church to accountability, many of us might not have looked back at all. Their resolution to call us all to accountability, repentance, and restitution has been the foundation upon which many other insights and actions follow; nothing compares to their efforts of standing alone for so long. The report then serves as a witness to what happened to them.

Looking Forward to Reform

The National Review Board does not simply look back. Like the organizations of victims/survivors, other lay organizations, priestly associations, and the bishops themselves, the board has been working to bring a variety of remedies to the fore. And while there still remains considerable disagreement among these groups as to which remedies would be best, all acknowledge that a variety of changes must take place to correct what happened in the past.

Above all, the U.S. bishops, in commissioning this report, in cooperating with the National Review Board, and in submitting their records to the John Jay study that the board established, have shown their commitment to making the church's future safer and more credible. Earlier, the bishops had demonstrated their commitment to address the crisis by adopting the Charter for the Protection of Children and Young People, which the report calls "a milestone in the history of the Church in America" (48). In implementing the charter some bishops have already established "model" diocesan lay review boards to assess allegations of sexual abuse (49). What continues to remain for the bishops to do is to take greater ownership of the report. That will not be easy inasmuch as the report challenges the bishops to weed out failures within their own ranks with the same dispatch they exercised with the clergy.

It is important to accept the report with realism. Its specific focus is to assure that the crisis never happens again, that children are protected, that no priest preys on children, and that no bishop fails to protect the minors in his care. Its specific concerns may color other attendant concerns. For example, readers might wonder aloud about some of the claims made. Bishops might find the report too demanding. Canon lawyers might argue that the defects of canonical practice ought not to prompt blaming the law itself. And victims' groups might wonder where they fit into the picture now.

Several times the report reminds readers of the then anticipated visitation of all U.S. seminaries in light of the scandal and talks about holding the seminaries accountable. But to what? Are there any causal connections between a predatory priest's actions and his seminary education? Could any standards avoid repetition? Could the crisis have arisen from what was taught? From the way seminarians were treated (too permissively or too harshly?), I myself am unable to understand the board's expectations for the visitation.

I think what we are still missing now five years after the report was published is why some dioceses at certain points had much higher percentages of priests abusing. What factors contributed to some archdioceses having a hefty number of pedophilia cases and others lower numbers?

Are the authors suggesting that seminaries work to create an atmosphere that promotes maturity, critical thinking, a profound self-understanding, as well as pastoral and theological competency? If so, that really does not come through in the report. Rather, it seems that a clear doctrine on long-standing sexual moral teachings, absolute clarity on the wrongness of violating sexual boundaries, and a fair amount of monitoring a seminarian's everyday conduct are the expectations in the report.

Nor do I understand why the board, which asserts the bishops' authority and still insists on bishops' accountability to the laity, could not propose similar relationships between bishops and priests. Priests deserve fairness, accountability, and even swiftness concerning their case if justice is the goal. And they need to become effective participants in the plans for having a more responsible church.

Despite these reservations, the work of this national board is one of the first demonstrations in U.S. history of cooperative lay oversight endorsed by the episcopacy. One must read this report recognizing its significance. It is the voice of an intelligent, competent Catholic laity demanding clarity, candor, integrity, and accountability of church leaders. The board's urging of bottom-line procedures and its bold-faced, respectful reporting stand as a model for church dialogue.

Moreover, the tone, the hope, and the vision of the report captured in its own words shows itself less interested in providing an indictment and more interested in helping the church look forward. In 2004 this was a strong indication of how the church could resiliently claim its future by acknowledging its faults but also understanding its rich legacy.

Building Up Tomorrow's Church through Dialogue

Other signs of building the foundations of a church for the future emerged again through promoting dialogue. The clearest instance comes from the Voice of the Faithful, which, especially in Boston, has energized the laity and clergy through a wide variety of forums designed to foster communication among all Catholics.

Lay initiatives are taking place elsewhere, such as development in relationships between parishes and apostolates of higher education. Many noteworthy examples deserve comment, but I must limit myself to two. The first was a conference, the papers of which became a book; the second is a multifaceted educational initiative.

In March 2003, the Saint Thomas More Chapel Board at Yale University hosted a conference and subsequently published the papers: *Governance, Accountability, and the Future of the Catholic Church.* Taking up the "looking back and looking forward" theme, editors Francis Oakley and Bruce Russett introduce the essays by asking: "How did we get here and where do we go?"

Among the papers are many by Oakley's colleagues in the field of history who look to their particular competencies to ask what we can learn from the past. But there are many looking to the future. The then bishop of Pittsburgh, Donald W. Wuerl, reflects in the keynote on church governance. Canon lawyer John Beal writes on how the church needs canon law precisely because the crisis has "ultimately been less about sex than about power." Theologians Peter Phan and Gerard Mannion offer perspectives on the church from Asia and England, Wales, and Ireland respectively. Journalists Peter Steinfels and Thomas Reese comment on the impact of the crisis, while the president of Foundations and Donors Interested in Catholic Activities, Frank Butler, argues for greater financial accountability to the laity. The priest and writer Donald Cozzens urges Catholics to face our fear about the many disordered relationships in our church today. And political scientist Bruce Russett considers two extreme models of church governance, monarchy and democracy, and offers a mean between them. Russett borrows from the late political philosopher John Rawls to propose "decent consultation hierarchies."

In 2002 Boston College president William P. Leahy, SJ, launched "The Church in the 21st Century" (http://www.bc.edu/church21), an initiative to promote "a forum and resources to assist the Catholic community in transforming the current situation into an opportunity for renewal." In the past seven years, the initiative has sponsored hundreds of major events. After an initial year of looking back at the crisis, the second year proposed possibilities for renewal. One conference was entitled "Toward an Ecclesial Professional Ethics," which examined the ethical training of lay, priestly, and episcopal leadership. Like the conference at Yale, this one at Boston College expanded the network of experts. Not only were historians, theologians, sociologists, journalists, and ethicists addressing reform but also leaders in organizational management were invited to participate. Such specialists brought the insights and analysis they use to understand, assist, and reform corporate structures. Episcopal, clerical, and lay leaders (such as Archbishop John Quinn and Voice of the Faithful president James Post, also a professor of management) responded to the presentations.

The conference asked, "How can Catholics promote/ensure adherence to professional ethics among church leaders?" It acknowledged that students at seminaries, divinity schools, and schools of theology rarely receive the ethical training required at other professional schools. Students at business, medical, or law schools take ethics courses that address the ethical issues relevant to their particular profession. They are taught the specific responsibilities and rights: matters of representation, confidentiality, whistle-blowing, client expectations, privileges, promotions, evaluations, conflicts of interest, professional boundaries, etc.

Such ethical training is even today, five years later, generally not found at most seminaries, divinity schools, or schools of theology, even though many students do take two, three, or even four courses in Christian ethics. They do not study the ethical demands of their vocation, but rather, the norms of sexual and reproductive morality for the laity, the social ethics of governments and businesses, and the medical ethics of physicians and nurses.

Students in ministry are taught how to govern and to hold morally accountable the members of their congregations. But generally speaking they are not taught by what ethical reasoning, insights, or norms they should govern themselves. Only in recent years have we seen the beginning of courses on ethics and pastoral ministry that highlight, I think, a new awakening within the church.

Still, regarding dialogue itself, the challenge for the clergy is somewhat different than it is for the laity. For the most part the laity, when they speak about the church, speak in horizontal directions. Like the Voice of the Faithful, they meet to discuss with one another the possibilities of reform. They are not formed by a hierarchical viewpoint, nor do they particularly emulate a hierarchical style. Priests speak, however, to their congregations and to their bishops, both in vertical directions. They are mindful of the levels or tiers in the church and with an enormous shortage of priests; they are even less able to talk with their peers. In fact, the attempts for some clergy to organize among themselves into diocesan wide fellowships have in many instances floundered. The question then becomes, "If the clergy need to be in dialogue with the laity, what would that look like? If they have hesitancies with fellow priests, how will they converse with the laity?"

Certainly priests have professional conversations as with parish councils, but when the priest is invited to friendship with members of the laity, to what extent does he begin speaking with them horizontally? Here a host of issues arise: privacy, parish decision making, the humanity of the priests, the maturity of the laity, prudence, etc. But like ethical formation, it is not yet clear how mindful most clergy are that such dialogue develops from experience and from an ability to share. Here the initiative of the laity as well as a few more experienced clergy might help other priests to get into a type of conversation that seems, in light of the other developments, a natural step forward.

Chapter Two

Proposing an
Ethics of the Word

At Fordham University, I taught for four years both graduate and undergraduate students. Later, in 1991, I began teaching only graduate students at Weston Jesuit School of Theology. There we had about 220 graduate students—lay, religious, and clergy. These students always had a keen background and interest in theology and the life of the church.

When I went to Boston College in 2004 I taught undergraduates for the first time in fourteen years. In my first semester there, I taught The Church and Ethics, one of the courses related to the Boston College initiative, The Church of the 21st Century. I had a dozen undergraduates and five graduate students, and a chaplain who had won a fellowship for her longtime service at Harvard University.

What most struck me was the undergraduates' response to the reading list. Whenever they read an account of a church official speaking in anything other than clear, respectful, and somewhat tolerant language, they expressed genuine concern about the speaker's suitability to lead within the church. They were especially puzzled by the way church leaders spoke at times in veiled terms, an almost secret language that only certain people could understand.

During the course they studied what the church is and what discipleship calls us to do. The students examined a variety of themes from truth-telling and authority to due process. They considered several major cases, from Galileo and the witch trials in what today is called Germany to the more recent cases of the scandal itself. Inevitably the undergraduates pointed out the importance of dialogue and honest speech.

I began to realize how important language is for the church and how appropriate it is, since our church understands the importance of the Word. I began to understand that good ethics for the church ought to focus on the Word itself. John's Gospel begins with that incomparable prologue, which invites us to see that the Son of God is the Word. We Christians celebrate the Incarnation, the Word made flesh.

In that mystery Augustine saw a moral mandate: the Christian should never lie because to lie would be effectively to betray the Word. Since we associate the Word with Christ, our words are important.

Still, the link I was trying to spell out is not solely about Christ, but it is also about words, his and ours. We understand from John's Gospel that a key analogous term for Christ is the Word; Jesus is God's living word in our midst. Because of God's self-revelation we understand that all communication is sacred—from Jesus as the Word, to the Scriptures as the word of God, to a language among ourselves where, when we give our word, we are giving our truth.

For reasons that will become, hopefully, increasingly clear throughout the next few chapters, I think that "turning to the Word" is an appropriate way of appreciating how ethics can help serve the church's mission.

An Ethics of the Word

Benezet Bujo, a famous African theologian, has written extensively on conversation and dialogue. Although he teaches in Switzerland, he has developed it from his own experience in his native country, the Democratic Republic of the Congo.

According to him, the basic place for this Ethics of the Word is the community itself. Every community needs, Bujo argues, an Ethics of the Word. Through this ethics a community can discuss, share, and search. Bujo claims that the end or goal of an Ethics of the Word is not simply to have a good conversation, as valuable as that may be, but more importantly to converse in order to help the community resolve crises, heal the sick, and determine itself for the future. An Ethics of the Word leads a community to fuller life.

The most fundamental ground rule for this ethics is that everyone must have the right to speak in view of building up the community. The community must learn to appreciate the uniqueness of each member. Here Bujo echoes Paul's acknowledgment in I Corinthians: that every Christian has specific gifts, gifts that differentiate us, yet we Christians are constituted in the one body of Christ. Our gifts only matter in community. Each of us must contribute to the community by offering our unique gifts.

The Ethics of the Word shapes the community, its leadership, and its members; Bujo calls his ethics a "palaver ethics," *palaver* meaning "word." It comes from the types of conversations that Portuguese colonizers had with African tribal leaders, who made "palaver" more inclusive and more immediately relevant to the community itself. They named their own tribal conversations that shaped the community's future "palavers."

Bujo develops the dynamics of his ethics as it pertains to leadership. It bears significance for all of us who seek to serve the church in its search for truth. Bujo describes how the palaver works. The chief proposes a problem to the community, initiating conversation by suggesting how he understands the situation. Then the community considers it. They mull over what he says, chew on it, and digest it. The chief is then obliged by patient listening to receive everything the community offers. Notes Bujo,

"Being a good listener and digesting the word are linked in general to Black Africa."

The African palaver, this sharing of the word, is where various ideas are offered and considered so that they can help, not harm, the community. This in turn presupposes that not only the chief but also all the other participants in the palaver have "large, broad ears," distinguishing themselves as listeners before they speak.

An Ethics of the Word trains a community to listen to its members, to let each speak, to appreciate each one's point of view, to learn that a problem is solved only by a variety of diverse voices, and to try together to reach a conclusion. In a manner of speaking, the conversation shapes the participants in it: the listener becomes the speaker. For this reason the chief's credibility depends on his listening so that at the end he conveys what he has heard.

The chief's decision is not then made by fiat, but by a shared deliberation. He may not cut off the palaver before it has concluded. Similarly, he cannot end it by a democratic vote in which the majority "wins." Nor may he trade off other options with different constituencies of the community in order to get a partial agreement. The conversation ends only when the consensus has been achieved, the talking has ended, the voices are heard, and the agreement discovered.

The chief then speaks, the last to utter a word after having carefully examined all the aspects of the problem. He speaks when the communion within the community has been respected and has grown. The palaver (this conversation) aims for the communion that makes the conversation possible in the first place.

Such conversations are not esoteric but concrete. Bujo remarks: "The Black African palaver model does not begin with abstractions." Rather, it begins with issues facing the life of the community. The matters it entertains are precisely those that are central for moving the community forward.

To Be Able to Speak Is to Be Answerable

Others have developed this Ethics of the Word and its ensuing formative conversations as well. For instance, the English theologian Nicholas Lash has described the importance of conversation in church life. He too decides to measure a community and its leadership by the quality of conversation that they hold. Lash roots his claim as a specifically Christian challenge precisely because we have been formed by the Word made flesh. He writes: "In a nutshell: the church is the community of those who know the fundamental forms of human speech to be conversation grounded in response to that one Word in whom all things come to be."

With echoes of Anselm, Lash emphasizes the possibility of conversation in the concrete reality as evidence for the possibility of a broader, ever more morally mature, conversation: "To be human is to be able to speak. But to be able to speak is to be 'answerable,' 'responsible,' to and for each other and to the mystery of God."

Both Lash and Bujo offer us an appreciation of our need to communicate as communion. By moving us to see how the Word forms and lives in our community, they help us to see that above all leadership is both a guardian of that communion and a product of that communion.

Last Word

When I taught at Weston most of my students knew, to some extent, of the significance of changing the language of the liturgy at Vatican II from a universal, though "dead," language to a locally familiar one. My students today may intellectually grasp that change, too, though in many instances their parents were young children when altar boys responded on behalf of a silent congregation to the pastor's "Dominus vobiscum." Language changed the way we worshiped. Not only can we understand the priest's prayers as he speaks to us in our language but also now we are called to respond to him directly. We broke the shroud of silence. Something happened to our communities of faith when we began speaking at the liturgy.

As my students remind me today, we need a similar change now in the way we proceed as a church. We need to come together with our leadership, we need to learn how to discuss, how to listen well and speak well, and to train one another in an exercise of the word. Then as in the liturgy we shall see the community reach a new level of communion and maturity.

Learning an
Ethics of the Word

When I was growing up in Brooklyn my dad, a New York City police officer, a sergeant detective in the homicide squad, frequently worked the 4 p.m. to 12 midnight shift in Manhattan. My mom was always home and, along with raising the five of us, worked part-time as a typist. One night around midnight my mom woke me, asking if I would come with her to the basement. She said that probably the house was "just settling," but she had heard something and wanted to be sure it was not an intruder. She held a hunting knife in her hand. Scared to death, I grabbed a flashlight, and we headed downstairs. We rummaged around but found nothing, checked to see that the locks were secured, and returned to the living room, safe and sound. Mom said: "Jimmy, you were very brave." "No I wasn't, I was scared!" "But that's what bravery is, being afraid but still doing what you have to do."

I was surprised. Going down the stairs had been traumatic enough, now my whole way of looking at life was different in light of our brief exchange. I used to think that if you feel good, you are happy, and if you feel sad, you are sad. Now I was learning something else about life, language, and descriptives that were more complicated than the simple feelings I had had. It was my first introduction to moral language.

Learning a Language

When I was younger, I didn't speak English. I literally spoke my own language. Baby talk, I guess it was, but baby talk at age two, three, and four can get alarming. Often, during my first four years, my parents brought me to the doctor, who told them to relax, that I would eventually start to speak in English.

Meanwhile, luckily for me, I had the best younger brother in the world. He understood what I said. Bobby, a year younger, spoke English like a two- or three-year-old, and in time served as my translator. "Do you boys want to go out?" Mom would ask. I'd answer in my own language, Bobby would ask me if he understood me rightly, and then he'd tell my mom what we wanted to do.

Learning a language is learning how to communicate. What I realize now is that my brother Bobby provided a bridge between my world and everyone else's. He helped me find my way to English. From a fairly closed world that even my parents couldn't figure out, he led me to a far more engaging one.

Learning language depended on trust. I trusted Bobby to communicate for me. Years later I trusted what my mom said about courage. Language, trust, and communication come together. One need only think of a story like *The Miracle Worker* to understand how integral trust is to language learning and communication in general.

Learning to Preach

Gradually I learned other languages. One of the best things that ever happened to me was learning how to preach in a new language. For the most part, my first Sunday sermons were preached auf Deutsch!

The story is short: After my ordination I studied in Rome with fathers Josef Fuchs and Klaus Demmer at the Gregorian University. Even in the 1980s Rome had so many priests that it was nearly impossible to find a parish that needed a priest to say Mass. So, during my second year in Rome I began looking for a way to replace a pastor in another country and found an ad for a parish priest in the diocese of Würzburg. I had taken a year of German in Rome, but I took two months of intensive German in Munich the summer of 1989 as preparation to taking a parish in September. Having finished my course work, I could return to the Gregorian later. Meanwhile, I was assigned to Untererthal and neighboring Obererthal in the Würzburg diocese.

The pastor went away every September, and for three summers (1989 through 1991) I replaced him. Untererthal had 800 townspeople, and its sister town had half as many. No one spoke English.

Early in the second September, I went out beer drinking with the women's choir from Obererthal. It was, as the Germans would say, a "sehr gemütlich" (very friendly) experience. After a few rounds one woman dared to say, "Pater, Sie sprechen besser Deutsch." ("Father, you speak better German.") I confessed that the previous summer had been a language nightmare, that I had no idea what I was saying or hearing.

"Ja, ja, Sie haben viele Fehler gemacht." ("Yes, yes, you made many mistakes.")

"When?" I asked.

"Wahrend des Gottesdienst." ("During the Mass.")

"For example?"

"You should say to us, 'The Lord be with you' and we say 'and also with you.' Then, 'Lift up your hearts!', ("Erhebet die Herzen!") but you said, 'Lift up your rumps!' ("Erhebet die Hachsen!")."

"What did you do?"

"We didn't know what to do!"

"What did you say?"

"We have lifted them up to the Lord!"

We laughed. I was learning a new language, and many Bobbys helped me to speak as they did.

No one laughed about my Sunday sermons, however. I had met many, many gemütlich people, but one couple, Ludwig and Ingeborg Herbert, and their son, Stefan, were like family to me. I needed someone who would patiently listen to my drafts of my sermons, so I asked Ingeborg if she would listen to them each week. She agreed. Ingeborg was perfect, a housewife, bright, caring, a regular churchgoer. I would bring her my text early in the week, and she would listen to me. Frequently, she would say, "James, ich habe keine Ahnung." ("I have no idea what you're saying.")

I realized that the more concrete I was and the simpler my insights, the better I was understood. Still, in order for it to be not just a talk but a sermon, I had to enter into the mystery of revelation. For that, I turned to dominant Christological images like the cross. I identified the church with the cross and its community as well. I explained how the cross supported us in our suffering and how it embodied God's unequivocal love for us. But I had to be concrete, referring to someone's actual suffering and what the companionship of Christ meant to him or her. In time I could use theology in my preaching while keeping my feet on the ground and my congregation awake.

LEARNING THE POWER OF THE GOSPEL

During those three Septembers, I buried eleven parishioners. These were the first funerals at which I ever presided. I made a point of visiting with whichever family had suffered the loss. My most affective experience was in talking with Anna, a widow whose only child, a man in his thirties, had died in a car accident. In the eulogy, rather than talk about her loss, I referred clearly and simply to the stories she told me about her and him. The Word preached consoled her. It helped build bridges, bringing us closer to her loss and to her hope. The Word, Christ himself in the Gospel, helped us enter into communion with her. As a preacher I saw more clearly how effective preaching the Word can be, how even in loss, the Word can stand as a witness to the empty tomb described in Scripture. I was learning the language of preaching, of communicating with my congregation about the way the Word of God lives effectively in our midst.

When I returned from studies in Europe to teach at Fordham, I traveled out to Long Island to preside at St. Joseph's in Kings Park. The phenomenally gracious pastor, Father Alex Manly, kept encouraging me and his associates to be concrete and accessible in our preaching. The Masses were always packed because the people wanted to hear the Word preached to them.

Letting the Word Preached Be the Place to Consider Word and Church

After four years at Fordham, I moved to Weston Jesuit School of Theology. When I asked Father Bill Walsh of St. Peter's Parish in Cambridge, where my Jesuit community was located, where I could celebrate the liturgy, he said, "Take my Sunday 5 p.m. No one comes! It's yours!" That was eighteen years ago. A senior priest in the parish, Father Dick Powers, had heard me preach at Weston Jesuit. After a few Sundays at St. Peter's with "no one" there, I approached him.

"What should I do?"

"Preach the way you do at Weston, it's mahvelous."

"But the people at St. Peter's aren't working for theology degrees."

"Make them wish they were."

It has been a moving experience. Today, St. Peter's 5 p.m. Mass is vibrant. More than seven years ago, right after the first reports of abuse by Father Geoghan appeared in the *Boston Globe*, one of our parishioners, Betty Anne Donnelly, asked me, "Are you going to say something about the sexual abuse stories?"

"No, why?"

Within a week I realized that the congregation wanted some Gospel way to think through the events unfolding in Boston. They wanted a light to illuminate them, a light the newspapers could not give. They wanted to see how the Word would be preached in the midst of a crisis filled with tragedy, hurt, and deep suspicion.

I learned that the language of the Gospel could lift up angry, fearful people, not with false hope (for Christian hope is always found near the cross), but with a hope rooted in Christ and his Word. As people wanted to have their trust restored, they found security in their faith.

I remember one Sunday, I preached on what it felt like to be a priest in Boston. I told the congregation about my experiences and that of my fellow priests. I described our anger, confusion, and shame. I talked of the hope of the Gospel and what it meant to be a priest preaching the Gospel when people were astonished at the number of priests under accusation. It was very well received. In the midst of all the silence and fear in Boston, I spoke of my situation as a priest. Instead of being alarmed, the people were comforted.

It wasn't about me. It was about being a priest in Boston. Here the people of God got a glimpse of what one of the priests was thinking, feeling, and experiencing. They were relieved to hear how one of us was looking at contemporary reality, especially through the light of the Gospel.

The revelation of Christ preached is as momentous as the bread and wine transformed, I think. The Gospel enables us to build bridges, to come to a new understanding, and to enter into a communion of hope and trust, which the Eucharist celebrates.

As we think about what we need to do as a church, we must not go outside of the context that we know. Rather, taking Betty Anne Donnelly's question as an example, we must ask how we as a church ought to proceed, precisely in the effective light of the Word preached in our midst. Since we have been formed by the Gospel, we need not fear to ask the hard questions.

Chapter Four

SILENCE IN AN
ETHICS OF THE WORD

After watching the impact of Hurricane Katrina striking the Gulf region, a variety of reflections surfaced: poverty, racism, tragedy, the environment, government preparedness and response. Still, before expressing any shame, anger, or even analysis, the magnitude of the event stuns us into silence, a key stance for an Ethics of the Word.

OUR HOMELESSNESS

One fall evening in 1990, after I had given a lecture at my family's parish on Long Island, I visited my folks. The three of us sat around for two hours talking away. A near perfect evening.

I drove back to Fordham University, an hour's drive. When I got in, I saw a phone message: "We're all right, son . . . ." It was my dad, coughing. "But our heating system ignited and destroyed the house about twenty minutes after you left. We are at your sister's house, but your mother and I are all right. I'm afraid we've lost everything else."

I called to assure them that I would see them the next morning. Then I sat down and sobbed.

Next morning I saw the remnant of their once beautiful home. They bought it after I had moved to Rome for doctoral studies. Now that their children were grown up, they wanted a smaller home, close to the beach. The first thing I saw was a sensational, full-length black coat that my mom loved. It was lying in the driveway on top of a heap of water-soaked, smoke-ridden clothing. Beneath the coat were her mother-of-the-bride (or groom) gowns from each of my siblings' weddings. Mom's closet must have been dumped here by the firefighters.

As I was looking at it, my folks arrived. They hadn't yet seen the destruction. My mom saw the coat and simply moaned. She went into the space that was their bedroom, looking for the drawers full of our report cards, letters, photos, and Mother's Day cards that she had saved. She saved everything about each of us: our first hair clippings, our first booties, our baptismal gowns. In shock she saw the chest with all her keepsakes destroyed.

My folks bought the house in 1985, five years after my brother Bobby's death at age twenty-six. They had wanted to rebuild their lives. This new house was different. It was in a wonderful location. My dad loved walking down to Sunken Meadow beach to take his evening stroll on the boardwalk. There was a restfulness about it. All of us loved my parents' home.

Now it was smoldering. My parents would spend nine months rebuilding it. They would live in a motel, where weekends were particularly awful: proms, weddings, and blowout parties kept them up every night. They were sixty years old and had lost everything they owned. After nine months they were happy to sell the house and move to Florida.

Eight months before the fire, my dad had double bypass surgery. So as they oversaw the rebuilding of their home, I made a point of driving to Long Island every two or three days. I watched my dad struggle; he felt so bad that, when they should be retiring, he and

Mom were in such a predicament. I urged him to take it slower. He said, "Son, I want to get out of here. I want to go to Florida and sit on the beach and hold your mother's hand."

They went to Florida and lived two months in a rental, waiting for their condo to be built. Then in November, about a year after the fire, Dad suffered a heart attack and died.

Who Understands the Loss When You Lose Your Home?

The day after the fire, my mother was going through the pile of her most elegant clothes in the driveway with no privacy at all. Drivers passed by, tsking. Heartbreaking. A pastoral associate from the parish drove up. Not knowing what to say, she broke the silence, "It could have been worse, Dolores; you and Frank could have been asleep and perished." "It would have been better had we slept; I wouldn't be here cleaning up this mess," Mom said.

Once the silence was broken, the vacuous words could not be retracted. The associate thought my mom unreasonable and just got in the car and left, unable to fathom my mom's sense of loss.

When Katrina occurred I watched the television, read the newspapers, listened to the radio. I kept trying to hear the narratives of the families in Biloxi and Gulfport. What can we say of New Orleans? There is an entire city of persons who in some instances lost their loved ones, but in almost all instances, lost their homes. An entire city homeless. A horrendous number of perspectives highlight the tragedy, but for me, the loss, the shame, and the sadness of the sudden destruction of one's home is my meditative framework.

I thought of Dad's phone message fifteen years earlier; it echoes in my ear as I watch one terrible story of devastation after another. I wonder, what was that woman's favorite coat? Where were their pets? What were their irreplaceable souvenirs? I heard one woman on National Public Radio just sobbing about her husband's lost journals and thought, yes, I know what that means.

Who will survive this ordeal? Which head of the household will collapse and die during the coming year? When will they get a good night's sleep, and where? What happens when a city of persons lose their homes? And which spectator will break the silence and say something completely useless, making the misery all the more ironic?

This is a time for action and response, certainly, and a time for pleading on the behalf of others. It is also a time for silence, and in that silence a sense of sympathy and solidarity.

Learning About Solidarity through Silence

I asked a colleague whether he thought that at the end of all this tragedy, we would think anew about racism, poverty, class, and leaving people behind. He said, he feared not. "Americans believe that a person's success or failure is their own. Eventually, after the silence, we will hear the voices saying, 'The people should have left before the hurricane struck.'"

I hope not. I hope instead that we think about these persons, not as makers of their own destiny, but as sharing in our own. I hope that by being silent we may come to a new understanding. There is, after all, something deeply transformative about silence. Silence is often respectful: indeed, often we communicate with God in silence (and God with us). In the silence we are with God. Silence prompts us just to be still, to watch attentively, to listen, to understand, to stand as a vigilant witness.

When I think of my mom going through her clothing in the driveway, I remember not even trying to offer her a word. Instead, what she and Dad both wanted from me was a respectful silence, that I would witness to them. In the driveway I was a sentinel trying to protect the silence that they needed and that I needed.

I think that it was silence that Jesus wanted in the garden. He wanted the three apostles to stay and keep watch, to be with him, not as interlocutors but as integral witnesses to his predicament. The silent companion is often the most appreciated one, particularly in the face of unanticipated tragic loss.

In an Ethics of the Word, we often should not be silent. Often we need to converse, to be in dialogue, to search together for a more honest church, a more just and loving world. But some events of great magnitude bring us to an awesome silence, allowing us to witness, to understand, to see humanity painfully, yet sympathetically. In short, by such silence we can identify with another and be the witness to their suffering, just as John, Mary, and the Magdalene were.

The people of New Orleans were entitled to no less, as they stood homeless before structures that were once their homes. They deserved the silence, the witness, and the respectful sympathy.

Part II

THE HUMANITY
OF OUR DISCOURSE

Chapter Five

THE HUMAN VOICE

At St. Thomas Aquinas Grammar School in Brooklyn I had wonderful teachers, the Sisters of Mercy, the Brothers of the Holy Cross, and several lay men and women. One of them was Miss DeVivo, who taught music. She began her first class with one question that mesmerized all of us: "What is the greatest musical instrument in the world?"

We fifth graders took the bait and immediately offered a host of responses: the piano, the organ, the flute. After nearly every instrument was named, someone uttered "the harp," and, quickly, we fifty-eight Brooklyn-born-and-bred boys turned to our classmate in a single move of disbelief to mutter astonishingly in unison, "The harp?"

Miss DeVivo, delighted by our animation (and cleverness), came to his rescue, by saying, "You're all wrong. It's the human voice."

We were even more astonished.

Miss DeVivo provided us with a "eureka moment," and we would never forget it. She subsequently explained the enormous, inimitable quality of the human voice. Speaking of its range, clarity, complexity, and flexibility, she convinced all of us that we had within each of us the finest instrument on earth. It was an incredible moment; the human voice was more polished, elegant, and fluid than all the eighty-six keys on a grand Steinway.

In this volume, we have been reflecting on an Ethics of the Word, an ethics that is built on the divine communication of God in the person of Jesus Christ, the Word made flesh. We have seen how many pastors, theologians, and lay leaders around the world have called for a new level of dialogue so as to cultivate a spirit of mutual respect and to secure a common ground. We have also seen that that ethics reveals the darkness of our community of faith when we misrepresent or bear false witness to our neighbor.

In light of our ongoing investigation, we need to take stock of the human voice, of that which utters the words of praise, of communication, or of slander. If we speak of an Ethics of the Word without considering the human voice, we will have a simple ethics of language. It only becomes an Ethics of the Word, that is, it only becomes embodied, interpersonal, and social, when we recall the Word as uttered through the voice. The human voice makes the Word alive.

The human voice connects us to the human person. I realize this whenever I decide to call a friend or loved one. I may look at their photograph or I may write them a letter or an email, and I may receive a letter or an email in return. But something different happens when I hear their voice, whether by phone or face to face.

There I hear the texture of their voice.

I can hear whether they are refreshed, upbeat, beaten, resilient, waking, retiring, running, driving, or sitting. I can hear their health, their emotional soul, their animated bodies. By their breathing, I hear their movement; by their voice, I hear their spirit. I can hear the lilt of their joy, the playfulness of their expectations, the desire behind their storytelling, the silence of their hurt, the success of their achievement, or the pain of their regret. A pause, a whisper, a laugh, a shout, conveys the multitudinous expressions of the soul uttered by the voice.

Recently I began a sermon by asking the congregation to think of photographs that they have of family members who had already died. I asked them to look at these pictures in their memories. Then I asked them to imagine their loved one's voices. The entire church changed. No longer were people recalling pictures of loved ones in nice frames situated in their living rooms or dens; now they were hearing the voices of loved ones once gathered in those rooms. By recalling their voices, they got closer to their loved ones. Now, their images were no longer two-dimensional: imagining the voice, they recalled their family members talking, breathing, laughing, communicating—in short, alive.

I told them a story about my dad's sudden death by heart attack, after he and my mom had only just moved to Florida two months earlier. I told them about a problem we had with her phone answering machine that had my dad's voice on it.

After his death we realized that we had to change the message: we didn't want callers confused by hearing his voice asking them to leave a message. So we deleted it. A deeply regrettable action, because it was the only recording of his voice we had.

I long to hear his voice, to remember the way he called me "son," "Jim," "Jimmy," or "James." He used each of these in different ways, at different times, for different purposes, but it was his voice that gave those names meaning. By the way he uttered them, I could tell the sense of joy or disappointment, frustration or gratitude. And now as I sit here writing this I imagine his voice, but in doing it, I long to hear it, for then I would hear him as alive, as "Dad," the only appellation I ever called him by. Just longing to hear his voice brings me closer to the one who named me.

No small wonder the frequency with which Jesus referred to his voice. We can think of Jesus telling us about how his sheep know his voice. We hear his voice and follow him. Most remarkable is that many of the resurrection appearances focus precisely on the voice.

The Magdalene is in the garden, weeping over the missing body of the Lord, imploring the man in the garden to tell her where they have placed the body of the Lord. One can only imagine her grief, confusion, and pleading. In the midst of all this, the gardener calls her Mary, and suddenly hearing her name from his voice, she recognizes him. It's not the name that triggers the recognition, it's the voice.

The same act of revelation occurs to the disciples fishing on the Sea of Galilee. They are working their nets off the coast. They see him but do not realize who it is. Not until he speaks, repeating to them the very words he uttered years earlier when he called them from their fishing to become his disciples, that John recognizes him, "It's the Lord."

We recognize one another by our voices. The phone rings, the caller does not identify themselves, but simply says "hello." We recognize them. We need no name. We have the voice.

The human voice, like the fingerprint, is a unique mark of identification. But the voice is different from the fingerprint, for it only functions when we are alive.

If we were to live by an Ethics of the Word in the church, we would need to recognize that the only way the church can be alive and grow is if it allows us to respect the members' voices and lets them speak. Our church cannot grow if we silence, interrupt, deride, misrepresent, or exclude another's voice. Those actions only cause us to diminish. But we need not only to cease those actions, we need also to encourage one another to speak; that is, we need communities of discourse or palavers.

Interesting, I find, that whenever I speak about the church and our hope for the future, I hear people in the audience wanting to express their pain, anger, frustration, and fear for the future. I am still surprised at the fact that so many have not found the appropriate occasion or setting to express themselves. At first, I thought that I needed to respond to them, to give them words of hope and consolation. But then I realized that people wanted and needed a hearing, they needed to be listened to.

I remember a lesson my dad taught me. When I was fresh out of graduate school, giving talks here and there, my dad traveled to a few of them. He was my greatest fan. He loved hearing me speak. But after two talks, he said, "Son, your talks are great. But during the question and answer sessions, you have the habit of interrupting your questioners before they have finished speaking. Let them finish the question."

"But I know what they are going to ask."

"Son, let them finish their question."

"Yes, Dad, but I know what they are going to say."

"Son, then, humor them and let them finish. It's rude."

I was surprised at how obtuse I was. I was not simply being rude—beneath my interruptions were an arrogance, a condescension, and a lack of humility. My dad was teaching me to be humble and civil, to recognize my place in the conversation. He was also teaching me to learn to listen.

I am still learning the importance of letting a voice speak. I learn this in the hospital, at home, in the confessional, in the office with the student. Finding our voice is key to our maturity, for we grow by our voices.

I especially urge my doctoral students to find their voice so as to mature into a scholar. When they find their voice they realize they have something to offer the church and the world. One can tell when a student submits a paper whether their paper actually embodies their interests and concerns. If the paper is not written in their voice, it's somewhat lifeless. It's an assembly of ideas; but if it expresses their voice, we can recognize the singularity of their argument.

Not surprisingly the literature that most frequently summons the need to give voice is found under the topic of pain. Of all the essays I have read on this topic the most striking one is on the voice and torture by Elaine Scarry in her book *The Body in Pain* (New York: Oxford University, 1985). There she argues that torturers derive their power from the voices of the tortured.

The most common object of the torturer is not to learn information, but rather to make the tortured blame her or his very self; the voice betrays the body when, so broken with pain, the body is unable to keep the voice from submitting to the fictive power of the torturer. The aim of torture, then, is to tear the voice from its body: "The goal of the torturer is to make the one, the body, emphatically and crushingly present by destroying it, and to make the other, the voice, absent by destroying it." The tortured body is left voiceless, once it acknowledges the torturer's "authority."

Scarry argues that the tortured person's most difficult wound to heal is the voice. To this end, Amnesty International assists the tortured, unable out of shame to tell their narratives, to read and understand their records so that they may articulate one day the truth of the atrocities. Her work convincingly demonstrates the centrality of the human voice in attaining healing integration. Together with other writers she highlights that silencing and other forms of exclusion are physically and personally destructive acts. Similarly she gives us hope that by letting one another speak, we heal.

As we continue to develop an Ethics of the Word and as we continue to look toward a rebirth of our church, let us be vigilant to the many whose voices are waiting to be heard. Letting them find their voices might well lead us to a new Pentecost.

Chapter Six

MEMORY

On the day my mom died, we found among her papers letters addressed to each of us, her children. I later learned from one of her friends that she wrote them several years ago. I do not know what she wrote to my sisters and brother as we decided not to share them. I do know, now, word for word what she wrote to me. I keep it in my prayer space, where I sit each morning.

There too in my prayer space is my niece Megan's memorial card. Megan fought leukemia for three years from the age of sixteen to nineteen. In her high school yearbook, she chose this inscription: "Promise me you'll never forget me; Because, if I thought you would, I would never leave." The words are on her memorial card. I begin my mornings remembering my mom, dad, brother Bob, and niece, Megan.

MEMORY, A SPIRITUAL PRACTICE

Memory is a deeply religious enterprise. For Christians, it is in the liturgy that we most evidently exercise in our memory collectively since the Eucharist itself is an effective memorial, especially as we hear, "Do this in memory of me." Shortly after that we often sing, "Keep in mind that Jesus Christ has died for us and is risen from the dead. He is our saving Lord; he is joy for all ages."

Through the actions of the liturgy we enter by our memory into the saving narrative of Christ. We see him in the breaking of the bread as we recall the same biblical instructions he gave to those on the road to Emmaus. Each time we do it, we remember him. And in the remembering, we await the resurrection.

But the liturgy as a memorial is not a one-way practice. For just as we remember Christ, we in turn ask Christ to remember us. We recall, for instance, the song we sing during the memorial of Good Friday, "Jesus, Remember me, when you come into your kingdom." These words once uttered by the thief on the cross next to Christ (Luke 23:42) are an appeal to be held in the memory of the risen one. Our appeal to Christ's memory is that he not only simply not forget us, but more importantly, that he keep us in mind. Our asking him to keep us in mind, to remember us, prompts us then to follow his command to remember him in the Eucharistic liturgy.

MEMORIES AS LASTING FOREVER

The practice of memory is an incredibly affective exercise. The Italians, for instance, use the word *ricordare* for memory; it means "bringing back someone or something to the heart." This exercise is affective then because it is rooted in real, relational histories. We can appreciate memory as affective by contrasting it with the imagination. Imagining the future is based on unseen and unknown expectations; memory is rooted in our connectedness with actual persons, conversations, places, and events.

Memory is, then, as three-dimensional as human beings are. By memory we can recall a smell, an odor, a scent; we can hear the tone of a voice, its accent, its inflection; we can recollect the touch of someone's hand, a gentle caress, a sustained embrace; we can taste a red wine, awaken to a spice, linger over a memorable kiss; and we can see how her hair was kept, the pants he wore, the flowers they loved.

Memory, then, is an affective bridge that allows us to be rooted in the present, to feel what once was, and yet to long for its return.

The bridge that memory spans is between our world and the world of glory. As Christians, we believe in the resurrection of the body. Though we do not know how it is or in what way we will see and be seen in our glorified bodies, still, it will be by our memories that we will recognize one another. I am not sure whether my hair will be as full as it is now, whether my skin will be softer or tougher, or whether my eyes will be just as blue as they are now. Still, I am sure that in the next life, I will have my memory, just as Christ and all in glory have theirs now. By our memories we will recognize one another again. Even more, by our memories we will know why we recognize one another.

For this reason, then, we remember those who have gone before us, not simply so that they may remain, in a manner of speaking, here with us. Of course, many times we remember those who have gone before us because we want to linger longer with them here. Still, we remember them so that we may be ready to recognize them when we see them again face to face. Our daily memorials, our practices of remembering are our preparatory exercises for the communion we long for.

Memory then bridges the deeply felt gap that separates us to-day. Just before his execution, on the eve of Hitler's own death, the wise and heroic German theologian, Dietrich Bonhoeffer, recognized in one of his letters the way God prompts us to remember so as to bridge the gap.

NOTHING can make up for the absence of someone we love—And it would be wrong to try to find a substitute. We must simply hold out and see it through—That sounds very hard at first but at the same time it is a great consolation, for the gap—as long as it remains unfilled—preserves the bond between us. It is nonsense to say that God fills the gap—God does not fill it but, on the contrary, keeps it empty and so helps us to keep alive our former communion with each other even at the cost of pain.

Memory, a Moral Practice

If memory is a religious action it is also a deeply moral practice as well. One only has to do a Google search for an ethics of memory and find Avishai Margalit's *The Ethics of Memory*, wherein he reflects on the lives of parents' families so deeply caught up in the Holocaust. Elie Wiesel too authored a similar book, years earlier, *Ethics and Memory*. These two remind us not only that we cannot forget but also that we must remember the Holocaust. We must remember so as to be vigilant to whatever could cause us to do it again, and we owe it to the victims to remember them.

For this reason we remember December 7th just as we remember September 11th because on both dates we need to remember our own victims as well and the villainy of such attacks. Still, we remember August 6th and August 9th so that we may remember that we were the first and only people to use nuclear weapons against civilian populations.

African Americans through their spirituals and essays keep reminding us too of the ways that we enslaved their populations. Lest we forget what slavery and segregation were, we are forced to face our histories to realize that the innocence of our being victims on December 7 does not translate into the innocence 200 years earlier of buying and selling fellow human beings. Memory forces us to remember white hoods, cross-burnings, lynchings, whippings, and the like. It reminds us of what we are capable and of what society can do, if we do not uphold justice and human solidarity.

Recently in South Africa the Truth and Reconciliation Commission tried to get an accurate history of events so as not to forget the history of apartheid and we see now, after its own horrendous genocide, that Rwanda attempts the same. Getting the narrative right is the key preparatory step for establishing an institutional practice of memory.

To remind his nation about the lessons to be drawn from their collaboration with the Nazis, the French novelist Albert Camus wrote *The Plague* and at the end of it warned his readers to remain constantly vigilant to the evil in our own hearts that can surface whenever we are least attentive.

As in all these instances, memory reminds us not only of the harm that has happened but also the ease with which a person, a people, or nation can perpetrate it. Memory allows us to not only recall the past but also to relive it. Because memory is so affective, inhumane narratives are harder to remember and sometimes we are more inclined to face such narratives without the graphics. In a manner of speaking, written accounts of suffering are more distant and therefore easier on the heart and the conscience. When they are contextualized by voices and images, the unfolding of the past approximates the actual past as it really was.

I often think this when I see a compelling movie about past atrocities to the Native American, the African American, the homosexual, the Jew, or some others. In some riveting and chilling accounts of how much some humans have suffered at the hands of others, I often find that the audience willingly acknowledges the lessons of accountability that the movie proposes. The people who "should" see the movie, however, are not there.

Here then we can realize that memory is elective. We can blot out our memories, or ignore them, or simply make sure we don't remember. In a very telling movie, *Crimes and Misdemeanors* by Woody Allen, Martin Landau plays a respected member of the community who, unknown to anyone else, is having a long-term affair with Anjelica Houston. When she threatens to tell his wife and family, he believes his singular option is to kill her. He is mainly dissuaded by this because he fears suffering remorse after the action. Inevitably he kills her. While sitting in a bar years later, he remarks to Allen that he feels little remorse because he doesn't bother to remember the affair, the love, Anjelica, or even the murder, and he adds, there is no one there to remind him, because no one knows.

Memory prompts us to take lessons from what we recall and reminds us today of what we are forever able to do. But if we do not remember, we do not remember. Like the spiritual practice of memory, the moral practice bridges us to the past so as to pursue a more promising future. But it is by memory that we discover the bridge and cross it. Without memory, often, there is no other link to the past.

A CONTEMPORARY SPIRITUAL AND MORAL PRACTICE OF MEMORY

Memory as a moral and spiritual practice came together in Boston on May 26, 2006, when Cardinal Sean O'Malley and twenty-two priests arrived at Boston's cathedral to do collective penance for the sexual abuse scandal. There they heard one abuse victim narrate his history; his account like so many others was precisely about events that earlier bishops and cardinals repeatedly urged others to forget and ignore. Now after years of denial and of deep refusal to face history was a call to repentance and a recognition of the archdiocese's powerful complicity in the harming of hundreds of children and their families.

In response to the victim's story, the twenty-three prostrated themselves for eight minutes in the sanctuary of the cathedral while a choir sang a litany of repentance, composed for the service by a survivor, enunciating the sins of abusive priests and of complicit higher-level churchmen.

O'Malley later visited nine other churches, realizing that without memory and repentance, there can be no forgiveness. These practices afford us the long healing graces we await, for by the practice of memory, we can have hope in the future.

Chapter Seven

CONSCIENCE

Though centuries ago Christians were known for the way we loved one another, ordinary events today show that as a matter of fact we are a church divided. Within our church we find ourselves filled with disagreement, and worse, distrust. The church suffers even more because of the way we categorize those with whom we disagree. With greater frequency, each of us sees other people as on the right or the left, restorationist or unorthodox, open-minded or narrow-minded. These categories allow us to dismiss fellow Christians' positions on any church-related topic with ease even before they offer their opinions. It is a debilitating, fragmenting, and unloving stance that is an embarrassment to Christianity.

THE NEED TO RESPECT CONSCIENCE

Developing an Ethics of the Word requires us to respect not only the opinion of each person, but also more importantly, to acknowledge and uphold the conscience of each person. Thus every time we enter into dialogue with another, we must consider that like ourselves, others think and hold moral opinions precisely on account of their consciences. No Christian dialogue is possible unless we respect the conscience of the other because each of us sees, affirms, and promotes the world of values, virtues, responsibilities, and norms through our own consciences.

Pope John Paul II made this clear at Assisi in the meeting for world peace with world religious leaders. On October 27, 1986, he stated,

> With the World religions we share a common respect of and obedience to conscience, which teaches all of us to seek the truth, to love and serve all individuals and peoples, and therefore to make peace among individuals and among nations.

> Yes, we all hold conscience and obedience to the voice of conscience to be an essential element in the road towards a better and peaceful world.

> Could it be otherwise, since all men and women in this world have a common nature, a common origin and a common destiny?

But conscience is not a simply a blank check that anyone can invoke as absolutely original and without any particular claim. In religious traditions around the world (as well as in the civilian life of most democracies) the personal conscience provides the moral material for interdependent cooperation and solidarity. Rather than validating any type of claim, religious traditions *and* the conscience uphold certain common beliefs. Thus, at Assisi, Pope John Paul II invoked two basic lessons shared by all religious traditions: the call to respect and promote human life and the call to pray to God for peace in the face of the world's daily challenges.

THE NEED TO FORM CONSCIENCE

The affirmation of conscience, then, does not mean that the moral point of view is subjective or individualistic. On the contrary, conscience is obliged to find and acknowledge the truth. For centuries, therefore, we have been taught from the Scriptures and the church about the basics of moral life. From the Ten Commandments to Evangelium vitae, we have received the teachings of what Scripture and the tradition asks of us regarding life, love, fidelity, justice, sexuality, etc. Our consciences do not emerge from an empty void but rather grow out of our experience of being born into a family and baptized into a church. From family and pastors, from evangelists and popes, we are constantly being lovingly guided in truth.

For this reason we understand the call to heed our consciences as first the call to form our consciences according to the Gospel and church teaching. We cannot make a moral judgment unless we allow ourselves to be trained in the wisdom of our faith. That wisdom teaches us that our consciences bind us always to find the truth and to love. Conscience does not exist, then, so that we can be free to act as we will. Rather, conscience exists as the summons to truth and love and stands under the judgment of truth just as church teachings do. Our consciences and church teachings seek to express the truth.

DISAGREEING WITH AUTHORITATIVE POSITIONS

While recognizing the important differences among people, the moral tradition recognizes too the need for a common respect of conscience. This has concrete application to contemporary life. For instance, we know that the late pope spoke frequently and strongly against the war in Iraq. He clearly opposed the United States' invasion of Iraq. But many American Catholics did not see the pope's teaching in this particular instance as requiring immediate agreement. They argued that the pope's position on this matter was not in itself as compelling as, for instance, the long-standing universal teaching that prohibits the direct killing of the innocent, which is the bedrock for church opposition to abortion.

In distinguishing one particular teaching from another, Catholics (implicitly) recognized the so-called "hierarchy of truths." Thus, for instance, we know that the teaching on the Trinity has a much greater claim on us than belief in limbo. We Catholics appreciate that all claims on our consciences are not of equal weight and importance.

Still, the pope's position on the war was not a simple, dismissible matter. He was not saying to us, "Oppose abortion and euthanasia, but think what you will on the war." As with his positions on capital punishment and consumerism, the pope challenged us not simply to consider his teachings but to heed them. When the pope opposed the war he was hardly suggesting, "This is only my simple opinion." Rather, his expectation was that we would recognize the truthfulness and wisdom of his summons.

So what gives Catholics the right to oppose the pope's clearly articulated opposition to the war? Do they have a right to oppose him? Or, are they "cafeteria Catholics," choosing to obey only some church teachings as opposed to others?

BEING BOUND IN CONSCIENCE

Catholics do not have a right to oppose the pope or to reject his positions, but we do have the obligation to heed, above all else, our consciences. For this reason, those who supported the war were obliged to obey their consciences, which presumably "dictated" to them the demand to go to war.

One of the most significant contemporary defenses of the conscience is found in the Vatican II Constitution on the Church in the Modern World, *Gaudium et Spes*. In paragraph 16, the council writes:

> In the depths of his conscience, man detects a law which he does not impose upon himself, but which holds him to obedience. Always summoning him to love good and avoid evil, the voice of conscience when necessary speaks to his heart: do this, shun that. For man has in his heart a law written by God; to obey it is the very dignity of man; according to it he will be judged. Con-

science is the most secret core and sanctuary of a man. There he is alone with God, Whose voice echoes in his depths. In a wonderful manner conscience reveals that law which is fulfilled by love of God and neighbor.

Interestingly, in 1968 the theologian Fr. Joseph Ratzinger wrote this commentary on paragraph 16:

> Over the pope as the expression of the binding claim of ecclesiastical authority, there still stands one's own conscience, which must be obeyed above all else, if necessary even against the requirement of ecclesiastical authority. This emphasis on the individual, whose conscience confronts him with a supreme and ultimate tribunal, and one which in the last resort is beyond the claim of external social groups, even of the official Church, also establishes a principle in opposition to increasing totalitarianism.

The commentary sides with the famous debate in the Middle Ages that occurred when Thomas Aquinas rejected the teaching of Peter Lombard, the author of the *Sentences*, stating that one should always obey church teaching. More than one hundred years later, Thomas Aquinas argued it was better to die excommunicated than to violate one's conscience. Later Aquinas asked, "Could we ever violate our conscience and not sin?" "Never," he answered. To disobey our consciences is to disobey our understanding of truth.

Still, Aquinas' opposition to Lombard does not necessarily mean that Lombard was wrong. While these citations point to what we refer to as the "primacy" of the conscience, it is important to understand the argument behind these claims. The simple one is that at the end of our lives as we stand in judgment we will be asked to give an account of our lives and whatever position we held, whether obeying every jot of church teaching or being more discriminating with its hierarchy of truths—in any instance, we will be held accountable for whatever position we followed. Inevitably we cannot claim that another forced us to hold one position over another; instead, we will have our own beliefs and actions attributed to ourselves and not to another. In conscience, we will speak and be judged.

BEING RESPONSIBLE FOR AN ERRONEOUS CONSCIENCE

In the *Summa Theologiae*, after affirming the primacy of the conscience, Thomas asks a very unsettling question: "If we follow our consciences and err, are we excused?" What does he mean by this? If we are obliged to follow our consciences and we do, are we still capable of being blameworthy for following an erroneous conscience? For example, say we firmly believe that capital punishment is right and in conscience vote for a candidate who supports its existence. Years later, however, it becomes clear to us that this is an excessive, unnecessary, and immoral form of punishment; are we responsible or excused from the earlier error of conscience? Thomas basically says, if we could have learned then that capital punishment was wrong, we are responsible for our error.

How could we have known this? We could have considered church teaching on the question; for instance, in Pope John Paul II's encyclical on life, *Evangelium vitae*. Or, we could simply have checked the teaching in the *Catechism of the Catholic Church*. Or, we could see the many statements and arguments in the newspapers about the moral arguments for and against capital punishment.

Similarly, we live today in a world of enormous inequality. Will we be judged by the economic suffering and hardship as experienced on other continents? In his recent encyclical, *Caritas in Veritate* (Charity in Truth), Pope Benedict XVI remarks frequently that globalization has changed not only the way economic structures exist, but worse, it has made the possibility of humanizing those structures even more challenging to attain. By the wealthier nations' construction of a distribution of labor that serves the former's needs for low cost products, the wealthy tier harnesses the poor in a world where equity recedes more and more. Are we responsible to be responsive to this?

I would say yes, and that the claim of being ignorant of these conditions is not valid. How could we not know?

These insights make the task of finding the truth urgent and rightly prompt our consciences to be restive. We must always be searchers for the moral truth, trying to understand human needs and suffering and to be responsive according to God's loving ways and teachings.

The best way we can find the truth is by leaving ourselves open to dialogue, humbly acknowledging that we may still not know the truth as we think we know it. One practice would be to leave ourselves open to those who disagree with us, for they will help us to see what in conscience we do not believe and vice versa.

Though right now our church is divided on many levels, those divisions could one day become instruments for entertaining a variety of perspectives for rightly ascertaining the truth. But that will only occur when we first recognize and respect the consciences of those with whom we maintain dialogue, despite our disagreements.

Chapter Eight

A CRITICAL CHALLENGE:
RECOVERING CHRISTIAN DIALOGUE

Ⅰn my previous chapters, I focused on an Ethics of the Word. I have done so mindful of the fact that since the writing of John we have known that the quality of our discourse is a testimony to the quality of our faith: anyone who says he loves God, but hates his brother, is a liar (1 Jn 2:9). We cannot separate our words from our deeds.

Even though later writers, like Ignatius of Loyola, would remind us that the love of neighbor shows itself better in deeds than in words, we Christians learned early on not to betray a neighbor by words. Since the time of John the evangelist and then Augustine, we Christians have learned that the way we speak of another Christian reveals whether we actually love God. The Word, the quality of the way we speak of and to one another, is a measure of our love for one another and for God. The two actions—what we say and what we do—and the two loves—of God and of neighbor—have always been deeply connected. For this reason, rightly, Augustine saw lying as a deeply un-Christian action, a sin.

We learned from St. Paul that we were not to use our language to be fractious. Paul drove hard into the Corinthians when some of them began claiming to be for one disciple while disparaging another. In his complaint, Paul did not insist on any uniformity of ideas. Rather, Paul targeted Christians who thought that attacking another's leader was the Christian thing to do. A good read of Paul's letters to the Corinthians teaches two fairly contradictory lessons: (1) verbally misrepresenting and isolating another Christian on so-called "doctrinal" grounds is usually highly un-Christian and (2) righteous Christians have been inclined to do this since the death and resurrection of the Lord.

WHEN BISHOPS SPEAK

More than thirteen years ago the late bishop of Saginaw, Kenneth E. Untener, wrote a compelling article about the way bishops talk about one another ("How Bishops Talk," *America*, October 19, 1996). I have read it at least a dozen times. Untener reviewed the written responses of five cardinals to two important position papers, one about the reform of the papacy by John Quinn, the retired archbishop of San Francisco, and the other by the late Cardinal Bernardin in launching the Catholic Common Ground Initiative. The remarks of these cardinals provided us, Untener wrote, "an unusual opportunity to look in on a discussion among bishops and see not only what we discuss, but how we discuss."

In each case, Untener found that the critics of Quinn and Bernardin at least implicitly misinformed their readers about the very positions of those they critiqued. Untener added, "I want to observe that in critiquing the responses of these five cardinals, I do not cite them as isolated cases, nor point to them as the chief offenders. I simply use the window of this public exchange to offer examples of what we all, myself included, do at times when involved in religious discussions."

Untener's second observation was even more stunning. He compared the discourse of bishops in speaking to one another as opposed to when they spoke publicly to non-Catholics, for instance, as in their testimonies to Congress. When bishops speak on behalf of the Episcopal conference or address important social issues, Untener wrote, "I would rate the level of discussion in those cases much, much higher—superb. For some reason we often shift down to another level when we deal with church matters."

Bishop Untener's account is not the only one. Another instance of how bishops "shifted down" in dealing with one another appears in Timothy Shilling's description of the hierarchy's treatment of Archbishop Raymond Hunthausen ("When Bishops Disagree: Rome, Hunthausen, and the Current Church Crisis," *Commonweal*, September 12, 2003). Shilling's account leaves the reader wondering what St. Paul might say of the treatment Hunthausen received.

OTHER EXAMPLES OF CHRISTIAN DISCOURSE

Leaders from other churches are, unfortunately, no different from their Roman Catholic brothers. In a book I edited with the Mennonite theologian Joseph Kotva, *Practice What You Preach*, the orthodox ethicist Vigen Guroian analyzed a debate in the Armenian church, which he describes as lacking "civility." One reason for the "baseness of the debate" was that "vital concerns over doctrine and identity were involved." Like Untener's and Shilling's articles, Guroian's described the Christian tendency to misrepresent the substance and compromise the basic standards of civil (let alone Christian) discourse, especially when bishops believe that something central to the identity of the church is at stake. Yet, as all three rightly note, precisely at that point church leaders ought to be more, rather than less, inclined to Christian standards of discourse.

And, as litigious as our culture is, this conduct is hardly an American phenomenon. In a talk given at Yale University's St. Thomas More Chapel, Gerard Mannion offered a euphemism for "shifting down" by recalling the words from 1964 by French Dominican theologian, Yves Congar, who forecasted a "haze of fiction" falling upon us. That "haze of fiction" stands as an indictment about the way we act. Echoing Hans Küng's argument "that truthfulness is a basic requirement of the church, a challenge to the church and, indeed, the very future of the church," Manion, an English theologian, reflected on the conduct of bishops throughout Europe. He observed succinctly: "Truthfulness has yet to be embraced as a default virtue in church governance."

At the same conference, John P. Beal, the canon law professor at the Catholic University of America, made a similar observation. "Although they are not the only rights of the faithful that have been given short shrift during the current crisis, the interrelated rights of information and expression have been conspicuous casualties of it."

These are not the flippant remarks of idle people. Rather, they arise from in-depth studies by recognized church scholars of significant decision-making moments in the life of the contemporary church. They are signaling in unison that in times of critical urgency our leaders' "default mode" is often "to shift down."

Moreover, these observations cover the past fifteen years, since Cardinal Bernardin raised the call for us to find a "common ground" for respectful discourse over orthodox theological disagreements. Since his summons, however, the quality of our discourse seems to have worsened.

This is sad indeed. Only twenty years ago our U.S. Catholic bishops' conference was world renowned for the quality of its discourse, particularly its publication of the major pastoral letters on peace and economic justice. After making their testimonies public and their drafts a matter of record, the bishops set a real Christian standard for right discourse. Times have changed.

ANY GROUNDS FOR HOPE?

I offer three grounds for hope that our church, together with our Episcopal leadership, will return to respectful Christian discourse.

Toward the end of his life, in 2003, in an address to U.S. bishops, Pope John Paul II reminded them that the quality of their actions in forging ecclesial communion would be the mark of their Episcopal authority. He spoke of the need today for each bishop to develop "a pastoral style which is ever more open to collaboration with all" (*Pastores gregis*, 44), grounded in a clear understanding of the relationship between the ministerial priesthood and the common priesthood of the baptized (cf. *Lumen gentium*, 10). This ecclesial communion also "presupposes the participation of every category of the faithful, inasmuch as they share responsibility for the good of the particular church which they themselves form" (*Pastores gregis*, 44).

He added, "a commitment to creating better structures of participation, consultation, and shared responsibility" should be seen "as an intrinsic requirement of the exercise of episcopal authority and a necessary means of strengthening that authority." Finally, he set a clear normative standard: "Every act of ecclesial governance, consequently, must be aimed at fostering communion and mission" ("Characteristics of the Bishop's Apostolic Governance," *Origins*, September 30, 2004).

Second, the later Monsignor Philip J. Murnion (who shepherded the Catholic Common Ground Initiative at the National Pastoral Life Center) wrote to the U.S. bishops just before he died in 2003: "If I were to sum up my final plea to you, it would be: 'dialogue, dialogue, dialogue!'" He concluded: "Permit me, then, with the last breaths the Spirit gives me to implore you: Do not be afraid to embrace this spirituality of communion, this 'little way' of dialogue with one another, with your priests, with all God's faithful."

Third, the Catholic Common Ground Initiative is already in its twelfth year. Its founder, Cardinal Joseph Bernardin, recognized what John, Paul, and Augustine did, that our communion is formed by the way we invite Christians into discourse and by the way we manage that conversation. For this reason the project proposed principles for dialogue that Murnion himself helped to craft. These principles help us to be witnesses to that ecclesial communion that we, together with our bishops, must now recover.

More important than any principles, however, is the witness of the leaders and the participants of this generous group. They, like so many others in the church today, are working toward a much-needed reconciliation within the church, and they begin it by appreciating the importance of sustained and inclusive dialogue.

Chapter Nine

Modeling Christian Dialogue:
The First International
Cross-Cultural Discourse
on Theological Ethics
(Padova, Italy, July 2006)

In the early summer of 2002, I was teaching as a visiting professor at the Gregorian University in Rome. A colleague from Boston College, Steve Pope, had just arrived with a group of students who were there learning about Rome. I asked Steve if he wanted to meet some of the moral theologians of Rome and proposed a dinner. I invited the Italian Sergio Bastianel, the Jesuit dean of theology at the Gregorian; the Maltese Mark Attard, a Carmelite abbot and professor at the Gregorian; the Irish Raphael Gallagher, the Redemptorist editor of *Studia Moralia* and professor at his congregation's Alfonsianum University; and his Australian colleague, Brian Johnstone. These four professors had each been teaching in Rome for at least fifteen years, and their two schools were only a mile apart.

Understandably, the conversation was lively, thoughtful, and memorable. At one point I asked them when was the last time they had gathered together as moralists and they responded, "Never." Fifteen years together, only a mile apart in the same city in the same field of work, never a conversation, or meeting, or dinner.

The evening's conversation and dinner in Rome gave me an idea: what would it be like if we could get together two, three, or four hundred moral theologians for a conversation and dinner?

My idea became a reality when I was approached in the spring of 2002 by a European Catholic foundation that asked if I would host a seminar of eight international scholars, who would meet annually for four years and at the end of the seminar publish a major text on themes in fundamental moral theology, for example, the conscience, moral decision making, the magisterium, etc. The foundation's representatives said, "Moralists today are so involved in the local church that they need to talk to one another across cultures. We need to host a conversation for these eight."

I suggested an alternative: give me the eight professors as a planning committee to host an international conference of moral theologians. They agreed and in November 2003, they funded eight of us from seven nations to meet in Leuven University, Belgium, to discuss the possibility of such a conference.

The meeting was fascinating; moral theologians from Brazil, India, the Philippines, the Congo, Ireland, Belgium, and the United States conversed for three days, and among other issues, we made five decisions. First, we all agreed on the need to hold the conference and articulated a mission statement. Second, we needed to guarantee that moral theologians from Africa, Asia, and Latin America attended, and we decided that we would have to raise considerable funds to sponsor their participation. If it was to be truly representative, we decided we would invite fifty from each continent. We would need to subsidize moral theologians from Eastern Europe, as well. This would mean substantive fund-raising. Third, because of visa restrictions and plane fares, Europe would be the best continent on which to meet and Italy the one with the most compassionate visa possibilities. We needed, then, to pick a city that embodied the intellectual and devotional lives of the church. We picked the medieval city of Padova, just a twenty-minute trip from Venice. Fourth, we chose a rather elaborate name: Catholic Theological Ethics in the World Church: The First International Cross-cultural Conference for Catholic Theological Ethicists. It was a mouthful, but it announced what we are about. Fifth, we needed to develop a program. Here we decided on four formats. First, we needed to have plenary sessions where we listened to the moral challenges on each of the five major continents. Toward this end, we had five continental panels (African, Asian, Latin American, European, and North American). Each had three panelists who answered the same three questions: what are the moral challenges on our continent; how are we theological ethicists responding; and what hope do we have for the future. Second, we needed plenary panels that could deal with the central themes of moral theology: moral truth, moral discernment, pluralism, and globalization and justice. Third, we needed to allow others to bring their agenda to the table through presentations in ethics as it is applied in the related fields of social, sexual, medical, political, and environmental ethics. We issued a call for papers and received more than 120 proposals! Finally, we needed a framework for praying, discussing, and reflecting together about where we are and where we need to be.

Padova would be perfect: a medieval city, with one of the world's oldest and most respected universities as well as the center of religious pilgrimage for those wanting to pray at the tomb of St. Anthony. This city where Giotto painted, Anthony lived, Galileo lectured, Harvey discovered the circulatory system, and Elena Piscopia became the first woman to earn a doctorate (1678), would be perfect for contemporary moral theologians. It was.

Having raised $450,000, assured Italian embassies around the world of the importance of granting visas for our participants, and presented our project to Padova's own archbishop as well as several cardinals in Italy and in the Vatican, we welcomed on July 8, 2006, four hundred theological ethicists from sixty-three countries, with 190 of these having had their plane fares and housing covered.

Our international conference was under way, with simultaneous translations into English, French, Spanish, and Italian. Notably the inaugural session was held in the university's Great Hall, where Galileo lectured for eighteen years, and there we reminded the participants that this was where Galileo invited us all to reconsider our place in the universe, the world, and the church.

WHAT DID WE GAIN?

What did this First International Cross-cultural Conference of Theological Ethicists yield? Let me suggest five important outcomes. First, as Padova's Archbishop Antonio Mattiazzo told us: it is one thing to read or cite colleagues from other countries; it's another to meet and discuss with them. This was particularly true for our junior scholars and our nearly fifty doctoral students who had read many of the participants' works and now had the opportunity to ask questions, to see what they were like as persons, and to tell them how their own work was proceeding. It was not simply a sharing of ideas; it was a meeting of persons.

Second, we discovered a lot in common, above all, that "we shared the same vocation," a comment frequently uttered. This was an extraordinary lesson and prompted a strong intellectual and affective solidarity among us all.

Third, with so much good will and respect toward one another, we were able to challenge one another. When three senior African moralists finished speaking on their continental panel, three African women moralists took them to task for not mentioning anything about African women, least of all that many still live in profoundly patriarchal settings. When a French scholar spoke of the primacy of the conscience, an Italian responded, speaking about the competency of the magisterium. Perhaps the most significant challenge came when, even after the North American panel spoke at length about the deep isolationism in the United States, its intransigence, and military aggressiveness, several others asked were we doing enough in light of the impact these policies were having in their own countries.

Fourth, appreciating the need to meet and dialogue spawned the formation of other groups. The Africans formed their first pan-African Association of Theological Ethicists, and the Asians explored similar possibilities. Women theologians established a Listserv after sixty of them shared a dinner together.

Fifth, above all the need to continue the dialogue emerged. Continuum press agreed to publish the thirty plenary presentations; Orbis agreed to publish thirty of the applied ethics papers. We pledged to meet again in four years; to establish a committee to work toward implementing organizational structures for our solidarity; and to develop a monthly newsletter (appearing monthly on our website, www.catholicethics.com) to keep one another in touch.

On to Trent

At the closing dinner of the Padova conference, participants encouraged us to schedule another meeting. Several added that we needed a new context: discussing local challenges was a great start, but we needed something more defining. During the dinner I turned to Renzo Pegoraro from Padova and asked, "Where do we go next?" He said, "Trent." This made a great deal of sense.

Moral theology became a special theological field through the Council of Trent; Trent was our birthplace. Trent is a beautiful, small city nestled at the base of the Dolomites, just an hour north of Verona; though everyone had learned about Trent precisely through the Council, few had visited. Trent would give us historical context: we could host a conference that would consist of three days: the past, the present, the future.

Planning for the July 2010 conference is well under way. We have a host of plenary sessions scheduled, and when we recently launched a call for papers, we received 290 proposals! The responses came not only from the United States, India, Germany, and Italy but from more than seventy countries, including China, Malaysia, Burkina Faso, Luxembourg, and Ethiopia, none of which were represented in Padova. Moreover, the leaders of the city and province of Trent are especially welcoming, making plans all the easier.

This will not be the second of three conferences, however. Rather, we are hoping that it serve as a defining moment to work on regional conferences. We want to instill in all the members a deep appreciation of discourse and an attentiveness to the catholicity of our global church.

Here in these two conferences we can see a concrete effect of the Common Ground initiative taken almost exactly thirteen years ago by Cardinal Joseph Bernardin, Monsignor Philip J. Murnion, and other leaders of the National Pastoral Life Center. They believed that conversation could foster healing, address misunderstandings, prompt reconciliation, and overcome resentment. Above all, they believed that conversation deepens and sustains communion and helps us transcend our own specific concerns so as to serve the church universal as she preaches and serves in every locality.

As we met in Padova, that same trust in the power of the Word guided us, as well. Now, the legacy of the Common Ground project outdistances its own plans as we await "From the Currents of History: From Trent to the Future." Such is the power of the Word and Christian discourse.

Part III

FORMS OF
CHRISTIAN DISCOURSE

Chapter Ten

TEACHING

In 1992, after my first year of teaching at Weston Jesuit School of Theology, I received my course evaluations. They were very affirming: availability, clarity, content, etc. But there was one frequently raised admonition: "Jim does not represent well others' points of view, especially those with whom he disagrees." As a junior teacher, I thought, "Well, why should anyone promote another's point of view if he or she thinks they are wrong?"

As my teaching improved and my defenses were lowered, I began to see this critique as a challenge. How could I bring others' viewpoints into my class? How could I give them a fair hearing? How could I still disagree with them?

Before I began to think of what I should do, however, I began to think of how I felt when I was misrepresented. In moral theology, this happens with some frequency in part because many of us have the tendency to reduce each of us to having one position or the other. We tend to divide everybody into one of two camps (is moral theology so oppositional?), and as a result we often do not really teach the specific contributions of each and every moral theologian.

A pet peeve of mine concerns dismissing someone as a "proportionalist." Like my mentor, Josef Fuchs, I have been a critic of proportionalism. This is a type of moral method developed in the 1970s: it determines moral rightness by weighing the differing values or disvalues in potential courses of action. I always thought this was an inadequate method and have spoken and written about my beliefs. How could one determine what actions had which values, and on what grounds did one weigh the differences?

Against both proportionalism and its more conservative opponents, I advocated a virtue ethics that claims that there are sets of virtues that we ought to develop, and we ought to take courses of actions that develop those specific virtues.

Still, in a variety of circles, any innovator has been labeled a proportionalist. So Fuchs and I each found ourselves being called proportionalists and eventually found most of our colleagues being described as proportionalists, even though most of us do not find proportionalism sufficient and have located ourselves in other movements (virtue, liberation, feminism, black Catholic, etc.).

If I did not like being misrepresented, should I not make sure that those whose work I teach are fairly represented?

I began to look at other viewpoints as meriting an affirmative action: if my students were getting so much of what I believed, then I needed to work harder to help them understand other positions as well, especially those with whom I was in moral disagreement. I needed to recognize too that my students, like myself, tended to reduce others' positions. Thus, I needed to describe other positions not only fairly but also I had to make sure that my students actually understood those positions. I took the approach then that I had to make others' arguments understandable *first* and *then* to critique them later (in my earlier years, I dropped the understanding and went right to the critique).

MORAL DEBATE AND MORAL DISAGREEMENT

Even though I began to represent other positions fairly, I realized I could still disagree with them. We need to have moral disagreement regarding political, economic, social, religious, and moral values and virtues. If we want to advance as a people, we have to be willing to entertain a variety of positions. As we do, we need to winnow out the differing claims, and eventually we become convinced of the merits of one stance as opposed to another. And we do not achieve consensus in the process.

Moral argument and disagreement is not easy. When we disagree with others, we are not simply disagreeing with a position they hold. When we hold a position, we identify with it and there is something, I think, in the nature of persons that helps us to understand why we each recognize differently the merits or demerits of a moral position. Each of us is personally inclined or disinclined to particular theses. Thus, we cannot simply say, I disagree with your position, but not with you. This is nonsense. In moral argument, we are disagreeing not simply with a position but with the person holding the position.

As teachers, in order to model moral disagreement, we need to do three things. First, we need to respect others with whom we are in moral disagreement. We might disagree with them and their positions, but human respect is foundational to all moral discussion and debate. Second, we need to practice a hermeneutics of suspicion about our own understanding of another's position. Too many of us think we understand an opponent's position, but we need to second guess ourselves and ask ourselves, "Are you sure that this is her position?" Third, we have to watch the passions that animate us into moral debate. We will see more on this later in the chapter regarding civil discourse, but because moral disagreement is so personal, we need to be attentive to the feelings that we have, especially those that could lead us to disrespect another by being dismissive of them and their arguments.

In time, as a teacher, I realized that the more I could articulate others' positions, the more I was actually confident in my own. There was a corollary here. I began to look back on my own tendency to reduce or dismiss others' arguments and began to see that this tendency actually derived from an uncertainty or an insecurity about my own stance and my understanding of the fundamental points of the argument in the first place. Not only was I insecure in my own positions and did not fully understand others' positions but also I did not understand the foundations of the moral disagreement in the first place.

I am sure that my own insecurity as a teacher prompted me to discard other positions that I did not bother to adequately appreciate because (don't tell me it's true!) I was afraid it would contradict my own. I think I am not unique in this tendency.

At the same time, as I began to practice this affirmative action of others' work, something else happened. As a new teacher, I answered every question that I was asked. Even if I did not know the answer to a question, I still gave some response that was at best an educated guess. Now, as I became more confident in teaching, I became able to answer such questions with the words, "I don't know. Does anyone here know the answer to that question?" Imagine that!

Finally, I began to recognize something else: the goal of my teaching was not to simply *inform* students of various positions. Now, I saw that I was to help them form their own understandings and to express their own positions. I realized that what I wanted most from my students was that they learn to develop their own distinctive voice so that they could become participants in dialogue about theological ethics.

I am not suggesting that each of us has a unique point of view that never coincides or overlaps with another. I am certainly not claiming that we each start at square one. On the contrary, I teach my doctoral students what one of my professors, Fr. Klaus Demmer, MSC, taught my classmates and me. In a dissertation or any other thesis, we enter into an already existing discussion. Therefore, before making our proposals, we need to understand and describe adequately the contours and contents of that discussion and then to make our own contribution. As Demmer would ask us: "What are you bringing new to what we have been discussing for years?"

COLLABORATIVE WORK, FORGING GREATER DISCOURSE

As I was helping my students to find their own way of expressing themselves, I began to realize the importance of inviting others into dialogue and extended conversation. I found, for instance, that I enjoyed collaborative projects like authoring essays and books with people like AIDS physician Jon Fuller, bioethicist John Paris, Scripture scholar Dan Harrington, lawyer and ethicist Cathy Kaveny, or fellow ethicists like Ken Himes and Tom Kopfensteiner.

I also took to working with others to edit extended conversations into fairly diverse collections of essays: with the Mennonite pastor Joseph Kotva the ecumenical project *Practice What You Preach*, and with the theologian Mary Ann Hinsdale and the Organizational Management scholar Jean Bartunek, *Church Ethics and Its Organizational Context: Learning from the Sex Abuse Scandal in the Catholic Church*.

At one point, I became interested in dialogue beyond our own national boundaries and worked on an international challenge, HIV/AIDS prevention. With Lisa Sowle Cahill, Jon Fuller, and the English moralist Kevin Kelly, we invited thirty-six Catholic moralists from twenty different countries into the book project, *Catholic Ethicists on HIV/AIDS Prevention*. How would we find these different moral theologians, and would they provide a variety of significant, informed, and respectful positions? Toward this end we developed three significant objectives. First, we wanted to show that HIV/ AIDS prevention was more than matters of abstinence or condom use. Rather, attending to the problematic contexts in which people found themselves was as relevant if not more so than other strategies. We wanted writers to address issues facing women, children, and the poor, coming from fragile democracies or those caught up in social violence. Why did these issues matter in facing HIV prevention? Second, we wanted to not be seen as challenging church leadership but rather as engaging positively the moral tradition of the church. We wanted readers to feel that they were in mainline Catholicism as they read our essays. We wanted to be very practical but orthodox, for unless we were both, we'd have little influence within the church. Third, on a topic that only a handful of moral theologians had already addressed, we wanted to involve many moralists who had not yet written on the topic. In order to get a discussion going, therefore, we worked to insure diverse opinions, from a consultant to the Congregation for the Doctrine of the Faith to the leading moralist in the Spanish language, Marciano Vidal. It took us two years of selecting people, but the work paid off: the book captured such an international perspective that it was reviewed in over fifty international journals, has undergone several reprints, and has also been picked up by Philippine and Brazilian publishers as well.

The Influence of the Catholic Common Ground Initiative

This attempt to bring more and more people into a discussion is, I think, the hallmark of good teaching. People want to know that a teacher does not try to indoctrinate but instead seeks to open others' hearts and minds to consider the different perspectives of any issue. People want to know that an issue, and not a singular point of view, is the object of a faculty member's instruction.

The lessons I learned as a junior professor, expressing not only my own positions but also those with whom I disagreed, helped me to see how far conversation can go when it becomes more inclusive. It prompted me in turn to teach and write with others. But it also helped me to see what I specifically was bringing to the discussion. By including others, I could locate where in the spectrum I stood.

No movement has encouraged me more on this ongoing dialogue than the Catholic Common Ground Initiative. That project, as we saw in the previous chapter, taught me to listen to differing positions, to respect them, and to encourage continued conversation. It also taught me to follow the instinct of fair representation of those whose positions I particularly take exception. In that, I became a better teacher, and my students became wiser.

Chapter Eleven

CONVERSATIONS

Being an Irish New Yorker and a Roman-trained Jesuit, I am a great believer in the richness and effectiveness of the conversation. I learned this first at home with a lively group of extroverts.

I grew more in the give and take of conversation as a Jesuit, especially during my five years of doctoral study in Rome and then the fourteen years at Weston Jesuit in Cambridge, Massachusetts. In both instances, I lived with interesting people who always prized the possibility of sharing concerns, values, aspirations, histories, and visions. In my community at Boston College, conversation begins in full vigor during breakfast when any number of topics is engaged before we each go our separate ways. Those conversations keep us bound to one another in a common spirit.

Some conversations have had a compelling impact in my life. I remember, for instance, having been at an impasse with my dissertation director, Fr. Josef Fuchs. He had rejected my first chapter, all ninety pages of it. Without any explanation, he simply informed me that the chapter was not my dissertation. Presuming that our disagreement was without any resolution, I began the process of resigning from the doctoral program. My spiritual director coaxed me into having an extensive conversation with my mentor. When I went to meet with Fuchs, he said, "I'm glad you are here." Over the course of the next two hours, we covered many topics related to the dissertation and therein I found we had much more in common than I thought.

Conversations fortify relationships. They help us not only to share different values and insights but also they help us to pursue mutual understanding. There's a certain gracious give and take to the conversation, where often we complement and compliment one another. Through conversation, we learn more about the beliefs of others, and as we articulate our own beliefs, we realize what we have in common with our interlocutors. And when there are misunderstandings, as there were with Fuchs, conversations let us discuss what was left unsaid.

Writing the dissertation went back on track and subsequently, Fuchs developed the habit of inviting me to his room with other doctoral students simply to converse about our lives and work. I will never forget those evenings. He would call me and tell me to bring two or three of my colleagues to his room. We would talk about all sorts of matters pertaining to the church and moral theology. Those conversations taught me to do the same occasionally with my own students.

Conversations also help to heal in the aftermath of misunderstandings. For instance, after an argument with friends, the very act of seeking conversation with them is often a formidable cure for broken bonds. These conversations allow us to express what often gets overlooked and often help us to overcome long-standing resentments as well.

The understanding and reconciliation that conversations accomplish are part of the "communication" of conversation. In itself, conversation almost always provides the opportunity for better or deeper communion. The words are not accidentally related: to converse is to communicate and therein to enter into communion.

Renaissance painters loved the motif of sacred conversations. In these paintings the Madonna is with her child and they are surrounded by (usually four) saints, who by being in proximity with

Jesus and Mary enter into a sort of communion with them. The motif starts in the mid-fifteenth century with Fra Angelico and Filippo Lippi, but nearly every major Renaissance painter did at least one sacred conversation: Giovanni Bellini, Titian, Tintoretto, Mantegna, Giorgione, della Francesca, and others. Often when looking at the work, the viewer would have no sense that any words are spoken or that any discourse is under way. But there is communication.

Sometimes, as in Bellini, a saint is reading a text and by doing so is studying the words of Jesus and Mary, or in another painting a saint is holding the instrument of her martyrdom and therein is a public witness to Jesus and Mary. But in each instance they stand together, and a certain wisdom exudes from their shared presence.

The Scriptures are filled with relevant moments of conversation in which communion is enriched and fostered. Think of some of those sacred conversations. What would it have been like to hear Abraham negotiating with God over the intended destruction of Sodom? What was the reconciling conversation between Joseph and his brothers when they finally recognized one another? What were the conversations between Joseph and Mary during the journey to Bethlehem or the flight into Egypt? When Jesus took the twelve alone, what did they really discuss? What did they discuss at the Last Supper?

Like them, we too engage in sacred conversations. Here I think of the *Spiritual Exercises of St. Ignatius*. Though they are held in silence, they are filled with conversations. While as retreatants, we are invited to converse daily with our retreat director, most of the sacred conversations happen within the *Exercises* themselves. In the first week, we are invited to see the Trinity in sacred conversation about the need to intervene in history and redeem the world from sin and death. Later, in the second and third week, we are encouraged to listen to the conversations between Jesus and the disciples as they pass through Nazareth, Galilee, and Jerusalem. In the fourth, we see the risen Jesus in glory, meeting Mary, his mother, and later the Magdalene and then the disciples. We are invited to hear what they say to one another in this glorious revelation.

Moreover, throughout the retreat, we are invited to enter into a variety of colloquies with the Trinity, with Christ, with Mary, or even the interceding saints. We learn to get into the habit of sharing with them our hearts and minds while waiting for their responses. We learn, in short, how to talk to and with God.

Of course, sacred conversations are exactly what prayer is about. Since we understand Christ as the Word made flesh, we can rightly consider the conversation as a near sacramental activity. For by conversation, we enter into communion with one another and with God.

Chapter Twelve

CIVIL DISCOURSE

Most of us learn at home from our families how to be civil. Our parents and elders help form us to be civilized, to partake in our culture as worthy members. They want to be sure that as we negotiate the world around us, that we do it with manners. Our elders understand too that we are a reflection of them, and so our public conduct reflects on them and on how well they raised us. For this reason, nothing is more insulting than hearing someone comment, "Didn't your parents teach you any manners?" The question is meant to suggest that an uncivil child comes from an uncivil family.

Not surprisingly the custom of manners derives, I think, from our understanding the fourth commandment. There we come to understand the virtues of filial respect and solidarity. Filial respect teaches us to regard our elders with a deference due them. This respect affirms their place in the community and at the same time our own. Solidarity marks us as related to our peers, friends, and colleagues. These two virtues help us to understand and maintain our place in the community. In this sense, they are deeply related to the virtue of humility, which is the virtue of knowing one's place in God's world.

For the most part language is a key mode for expressing manners and civility. I learned this when I began learning Italian to prepare for my graduate studies in Rome. One day our teacher explained to us the art of making a purchase in Rome. When you go into a shop in Rome and you want to buy something, say chewing gum, you don't say, "Chewing gum," nor is "Chewing gum, please" adequate. She explained that when you first walk in and the owner might be walking around or looking for something, you say nothing until the owner is ready to greet you, and then you greet the owner, "Good morning." Wait for her or his response. "You are after all," she explained, "in the owner's store."

"Then, do I ask for the chewing gum?"

"No, then, after you receive the owner's greeting, you ask 'How are you?'"

"What if I don't know the owner?"

"You can always ask anyone, 'how are you?' It's a question of concern, even for the stranger."

"Then, do I ask for the chewing gum?"

"Well, yes, but remember you just asked how the owner is doing . . . she or he might take some time telling you how they are."

"OK, after I get the whole health and economic history of the owner, I ask for chewing gum?"

"Well yes, but then you must ask for it in the subjunctive."

"You mean I don't say, 'Chewing gum, please,' but rather, 'Could I please have a pack of chewing gum?'"

"Exactly!"

In learning another language, I learned how every language has its practices of civility. I began to realize that ritual and language work together in the most ordinary situations in trying to promote filial respect, humility, and solidarity. For instance, as in many continental European languages, German, French, Spanish, and Italian, for instance, there are different conjugations to distinguish between the formal and the informal. Formal verb forms and pronouns need to be learned so as to speak with persons whose age, rank, seniority, or social position commands formal respect. To speak informally to a professor, a police officer, an elder, a priest, or a physician is not only rude, it is uncivil. Similarly, one uses the formal with one's colleagues, maintaining, if you will, a professional status.

One can only use the informal when a certain level of familiarity exists. Parents and children use the informal as do friends, and wonderfully, in the liturgy, the informal is always used in addressing God, such is our intimacy with God. These language practices are meant to develop in us a conscious awareness of how we are related to one another.

In English we have conventions that teach us the same lessons. We have formal and informal ways of speaking. If we are lost and need directions, we don't shout to a stranger, "Where's Lincoln Street?" Rather, we approach them, saying, "Excuse me, but I'm lost; would (that lovely subjunctive) you know where Lincoln Street is?" When we approach an elder whom we don't know but with whom we must still speak, we normally begin by saying "Excuse me, sir." Just as manners call for filial respect through formality, similarly manners call for solidarity through informality. So when we enter a restaurant and our host asks how we are, we reciprocate with a similar question about their welfare. Meeting strangers and elders requires a degree of mutual respect and civility.

These are not private but rather social practices. For instance, here at Boston College, I was surprised when I first arrived here how people wait and hold the door for someone. It is a very social act. It is not simply occasional that someone holds the door for someone following from behind, it's expected, and it happens about 95 percent of the time. It creates on our campus an inner disposition, that no matter where I'm going, I should be mindful of the person following behind me. I should make their passage smooth, just as the person preceding me is doing as well. Similarly, if someone is filing up the stairs and inadvertently runs into another, the words, "I'm sorry," or "Excuse me, please" roll right off the student's lips. Civility has a real feel to it here.

These are not superficial practices; they are part of the interiorized manners of a school community. For this reason whenever intolerant words are spoken, they are summarily addressed by the university community. These admonishing practices similarly promote respect and solidarity.

Manners can never be used superficially, for indeed, whenever they are we recognize immediately their hypocrisy. True manners are not superficial cover-ups of disdain. Rather, they are practices that are meant to train us in interpersonal exchanges and discourse. They are essential for the well-being of community.

In civil society and in the church I think we could do more to promote manners. One Sunday, for instance, a fellow priest told me that after the period of reflection following his homily, he mistakenly began the prayers of the faithful. From the midst of the congregation, a man shouted out "the Creed, say the Creed." The comment was filled with and illustrative of profound dissonance.

As in this instance, usually when we suspend manners, it comes from a sense of superiority. When we believe that we are righteous, or "smarter," or "more orthodox," we begin to think that we are not required to treat another with civility, respect, and humility. This, of course, is why my dad wanted me to hear out my questioners. He wanted me to drop my sense of superiority and enter *into* the community rather than to stand over and above it. Manners help us to be humble and respectful. We need them because we do have a tendency toward superiority; we need to check and discipline ourselves with these practices.

Still, we deceive ourselves, as when we don't hold the door for the person behind us, because our time is more important. Worse, we can believe that we should dismiss or deride the position of another, without having taken the time to read and understand the position in the first place. Feeling righteous, we believe we do not need the discipline of civility.

My friend John O'Malley begins the liturgy reminding us that the Lord loves the company of sinners. Real sinners know they need to be respectful, humble, and civil; real sinners know communally that they are called around the Eucharistic table. Manners promote within the community of sinners the virtue of mutual respect.

As I noted earlier in the book I edited with Joseph Kotva, *Practice What You Preach: Virtues, Ethics, and Power in the Lives of Pastoral Ministers and Their Congregation*, Vigen Guroian, the moral theologian, contributed an essay illustrating the lack of manners among hierarchy and clergy in his Armenian church. His words, I think, are fitting to close on, leading us to see how integral the language of civility is.

> Manners and morals in the church are not merely matters of decorum and externals of behavior. Their breakdown affects the evangelical witness and mission of the church . . . Where fundamental beliefs and matters of belonging are at issue, passions are bound to run high. Those whom the church invests with solemn responsibility to transmit and sometimes defend Christian beliefs and identity should receive a training that cultivates virtues of humility, temperance, and forbearance.

He adds, "But this type of training is desperately lacking at present in the preparation of Armenian clergy" ("Doctrine and Ecclesiastical Authority," 262). His admonition to the Armenian clergy is one we can, I think, take upon ourselves.

Chapter Thirteen

Being Called

Forty years ago, the notion of a vocation seemed only to refer to the call of a person to become clergy or a vowed religious. In more recent times, we hear all sorts of people describe their entry into their own profession as a calling. Whether becoming director of religious education, a lay minister, a teacher, a nurse, or a physician, people have grown familiar with the language of vocation. They use it to describe how they got where they are.

The language of vocation is a very particular type of language. It basically means that I am living this way because I have been summoned by someone else. Rather than saying that I chose to be a Jesuit or a priest, the language of vocation suggests that someone else did the choosing: the one who called. It has great social connotations: my state of life is not a private matter, but a public, social one. It is like a commissioning—I got called, and I got appointed. But behind all this, then, is a way of saying that I am what I am not by choice, but by response. I belong in this field, because someone else thought I should be called. Someone else initiated a conversation with me that has become lifelong.

Five years ago I was teaching at Loyola School of Theology at the Ateneo de Manila. Arriving in Manila is quite an experience. It's hot and humid, on a scale that most Americans cannot fully appreciate. The Filipinos, however, develop a way of living with the heat that includes a large measure of agreeableness. They rarely get angry. Sociologists call it "SIR," "Smooth Interpersonal Relationships." You arrive at the airport, hop in a car, and soon find yourself in five lanes of traffic in only three paved lanes. No one moves, no one honks, everyone smiles. Patience radiates across the lanes.

I was invited to preside at a liturgy for the Jesuit community in formation. There were about forty young Jesuits all in various stages of formation, and the first reading was the dramatic call of Moses where he encountered the burning bush. Moses heard himself being summoned. For the homily, I decided to share with them two key experiences of being called.

As a boy, I first wanted to become a farmer. Inasmuch as I grew up in Brooklyn, the first born of five, to a police officer and a secretary-homemaker, this was a strange desire. With three million people in the county, there were very few rural indications in sight. Eventually, my parents persuaded me that I had a very romanticized view of farming (was it *Lassie, Bonanza, Big Valley*, who knows?). I remember they kept telling me that I would hate the hours and the revenue.

Then, I became convinced that I wanted to become a priest. I had no idea of what type of priest I would become. Much as I liked the priests in my parish, I knew that I did not want to be a diocesan priest because as a priest, I hoped to move to different places and the diocesan priest usually moved, at best, across town. So I looked in the back of Catholic magazines for advertisements about religious orders; I cut them out and mailed them in. As I look back on this activity at thirteen, I think, how many thirteen-year-olds were doing things like this?

Eventually, the orders began to send me all sorts of information, to say nothing of second-class relics, invitations to novenas, etc. I contacted a few missionary orders but then realized, if the diocesan priests don't move much, the missionaries went too far. I wanted something in between.

When I received a response from the Jesuits, my parents said, "They're a teaching order." I quickly threw out the Jesuit packet; I wanted to be a priest and a preacher, not a teacher. I began thinking of religious orders who worked with the poor in the United States. I looked at the Trinitarians down in Virginia, but they were fairly southern in their sensibilities and I was clearly a New Yorker. I just about gave up.

Later, my family moved to Long Island. At my high school, which was brand new, I organized a Christian Life Community (CLC), and every Wednesday afternoon I led forty of my classmates to work in a reading clinic in a neighboring town. A CLC lay leader from a neighboring town, Ray Zambito, was impressed with our program and invited me to go with him by car to the annual CLC Convention to be held that year in St. Louis. Four of us drove two days to the conference; we were joined by a nun and a Jesuit priest from New York, Father Frank Drolet. Each of us would get elected at the convention (I became the board's high school representative) and through CLC, I began to meet other Jesuits.

Still, those days driving to and from the convention allowed me to talk at length with a priest for the first time. Drolet was saying things about the Jesuits, about how extensive their works were, how innovative their formation was, and how imaginative individual members were. Behind all these words was a spirituality I had never known.

When I got back to Long Island I began thinking about the Jesuits. Finally, one night, unable to sleep, I wrote to Drolet, a long letter with many, many questions about the Jesuits. Instead of answering my questions, he invited me into New York to visit him and in this way, at sixteen, I began a conversation with him. After several visits to New York he introduced me to the Jesuit vocation director. I liked what I was learning and whom I was meeting. A year later I would be a Jesuit novice.

The second "calling" occurred some time later. As a Jesuit scholastic, I planned on becoming a priest who would work in the inner city. A year before my ordination, my superior called to inform me that I was to do a doctorate. This was, for me, totally out of the blue. No one had ever brought this up to me. Stupefied, I asked, "What should I get a doctorate in?" After wrangling over a number of fields, he said, "You decide, but I want you to get a doctorate."

After asking friends what area I should go into, one said, "Moral theology." Why? "You get always get an A in moral theology." It wasn't the most lofty factor in a decision that would completely shape my life, but it made sense. In moral theology, I had studied with Sr. Mary Emil Penet, Lisa Cahill, David Hollenbach, and Ed Vacek, and in each course I did well. My papers were good, I enjoyed them, and occasionally I actually had a new idea.

Then, where would I study? I asked Dick McCormick for advice: Study with Bruno Schueller in Muenster. Yikes! Classes in German. Others suggested I look at Rome's Gregorian University, where Father Josef Fuchs was. My choice came down to courses in Italian with Fuchs or in German with Schueller.

One of my professors, John O'Malley, saw that I did not know how to get further in my decision making. Then he asked me two questions that would immeasurably change my life. What is the difference between Schueller and Fuchs? I responded, "Both are equally good; Fuchs was Schueller's mentor." Then, came the next, "Then chose between Muenster, a small town where you will be speaking German for five years, or living in the heart of Rome." The choice was made in the question.

These two decisions defined my life. Yet, they did not look terribly like Moses' call, from the burning bush, to say nothing of the calls of Abraham, Jacob, Saul, or David. Those were great calls: a summons from God, a wrestling angel, an arresting dream, a prophet's anointing. In each call, they did nothing, God did everything.

My stories were nothing like theirs. My first search was as a boy—my questions were naïve and my central one revolved around how far would I travel.

Later, I would be forced to make another decision. But did I discern any better? On the eve of my ordination, after eleven years of Jesuit training, how did I try to determine what God wanted of me? What did it all come down to? Grades and pasta?

My narratives seem commonplace, ordinary—I dare say banal. Yet as I look back, I see something else.

I believe that many people's narratives of their lifetime decisions probably look more like mine and less like Moses'. I dare say that Moses' actual call was probably a lot less dramatic than a burning bush. I proposed this in my homily in Manila, and when I said this to the Filipino Jesuits they all smiled, not simply, this time, because of "SIR," but rather because they felt if my narrative was so banal, they could live with theirs.

My candor freed them to deromanticize their own narratives of call. It let them familiarize and humanize the stories and made them accessible and attractive. In turn, they did tell their stories, speaking about their vocation and decision making in the same ordinary, fallible ways that I did.

Still, as I think back on these two decisions, I want to put them into two theological contexts, one from John and another from Paul.

I think of my vocation as conforming to those from the Gospel of John. In the other Gospels, Jesus takes all the initiative: he sees the fishermen, Andrew, Peter, James, and John, and calls them. After the call, they follow him. The Gospel of John, however, conveys a much more complex staging of vocation. First, the Baptizer tells two of his disciples that Jesus is the "Lamb of God." Immediately, without being called, they follow Jesus, and when he asks them what do they want, they respond, "Where are you staying?" Jesus invites them to "come and see." A second "calling" occurs just after this when Jesus "found Philip" and instructs him to "follow him." Later, Philip extends to Nathaniel the invitation to "come and see." The third "calling" occurs when Nathaniel wonders aloud whether anything good could come out of Nazareth and Jesus, if you will, surprises him, by telling Nathaniel that he has been watching him. Nathaniel is amazed at how well Jesus knows him.

Earlier in my formation a wise friend showed me how these three calls were three stages of awareness about the same call. First, the disciples think that *they* searched out Jesus; then, they realize that as a matter of fact, they did not pursue Jesus, *Jesus* summoned them. Finally, they realize that all along Jesus was with them, watching and prompting them way before they ever heard the call.

My teenage search came from the one who companioned me, and when I asked some questions, I was always met with, "come and see."

From Paul I learned another lesson. It's not the way I made my decision; it's the fact that God was guiding me through my own banality. God knew what God was working with and I was led, in both instances, by my own desires. It's why Paul's confidence in the Philippians (1:6) is so consoling: "I am confident of this, that the one who began a good work in you, will continue to complete it until the day of Christ Jesus."

As a Jesuit for thirty-nine years, a priest for twenty-seven years, and a theologian for twenty-two, I am sure of one thing: God knows how I got here.

Chapter Fourteen

TAKING VOWS

I entered the New York Province of the Society of Jesus thirty-nine years ago. I entered on August 17, 1970, at the age of seventeen. I cannot imagine that I did that so long ago. I can remember getting there, I can remember what the community was like, I can remember my rooms for those two years (we changed nearly every semester!), but I cannot remember much about the weeks that preceded my going to the Jesuit novitiate.

I am the oldest in my family, and my leaving was incredibly hard for everyone. Oddly, I cannot remember talking to anyone about the matter. I'm sure that my mom and dad knew about it because I would take the train into New York from our home in Long Island to see first Father Drolet several times, then the vocation director, and finally the interviewers and examiners. I do not remember talking to my brothers and sisters, in part because our home conversations were almost always through my mom and dad. I do not remember going to any sibling's room to say good-bye or to promise to write or anything like that. Years later I learned that the two youngest ones, Jean and Sean, who were only seven and eight years old at the time, thought I had left the family because of unhappiness.

What I remember before entering the Jesuits is the profound sadness I felt about leaving my family. In that sadness I made the decision that my family could not drive me from Long Island to Syracuse. We would never have made it; at some point my folks, sadder than I was, would talk me into not entering. So I bought a plane ticket and as I waved good-bye to my family, I remember sitting on the plane and sobbing uncontrollably. Later, after being in the novitiate for about five weeks, I called my mother, saying I was very homesick: "You can't come home now, give it a chance."

On August 17, there were five of us arriving in Syracuse from different parts of the province. This was my novitiate class, and I was easily the youngest.

In time my family began to understand more and more about the Jesuits: they visited me in Syracuse and I visited them on Long Island. Within two years I was living at Fordham University, a ninety-minute drive away from my family. There at Fordham I took my first vows in 1973. By that time, three of the men I entered with had left the Jesuits (and two years later the remaining fellow left as well).

Like all Jesuits I recited the vow formula that we have used for more than 450 years. I pledged poverty, chastity, and obedience, a public pledge that others witnessed to.

It was rather remarkable taking those vows at twenty years of age. I remember my family being there, my father choking up, my mom looking beautiful, and me with long, long hair. As I look back on it, however, I think of how many of the guys before me and after me left the Jesuits. In time it was pretty lonely.

During my four years as an undergraduate at Fordham I learned a lot about friendship and became a good friend with a Jesuit in the year behind me. We were both activists; I was more extroverted than he, but we were very good friends. I went away to Buffalo to regency in 1976 (years of apostolic work that are part of formation). After several months I returned to Fordham for a few days of vacation. I was looking forward to seeing my friend. A few minutes after I sat down with him, he told me that he was leaving. I was shattered.

After regency I went to Weston Jesuit for three years and then on to Rome. While I was in Rome, I wrote to Jesuit friends from Weston. I only heard from one of them and that was because he was really miserable in his graduate studies.

When I returned to Fordham, I became friends with the most hilarious Jesuit I ever met. We started at Fordham the same year and every night went for a walk around the campus. When I left Fordham after four years to teach at Weston, he was very hurt and it took years to repair the damage. Last year he was a visiting professor here and we were back on familiar footing.

Like many other priests, Jesuits are terrific when you are living with them. In fact, because we have vows—that is, because we are Jesuits—we know that each of us will be welcomed into any community in any part of the world with a familial hospitality. All of us know that wherever there is a Jesuit community, we have found our home.

Few Jesuits, however, maintain long-standing friendships. There are probably many reasons for this. A few of them are first, Jesuits make much of saying that we enter primarily for the apostolic work, and only secondarily for community work. Second, we are enormously mobile and the time it takes to develop a sustained friendship is often challenged by a reassignment somewhere else. Third, we are a fairly autonomous crowd, and I would not be surprised that that autonomy (like my own) leads each of us into the Society. Fourth, we were during our formation dissuaded from being friends with one person in the event we were to become exclusive. Fifth, by our spirituality we are companions of Jesus; the reliance on the Lord in friendship is quite palpable.

Living at Boston College now, I have a few friends in the city, including two Jesuits here. One is incredibly faithful to his friends and has maintained long-standing friendships over the years with several Jesuits. Strangely, I have never been jealous of these friendships, but rather comforted by them. When he gets reassigned in two years, I know I will become one among his friends hearing from him through skype and email. He will always be my friend. The other Jesuit will grow old with me, at Boston College. They are, along with my siblings and Maura, to whom I dedicate this book, my closest friends.

I write about this because I understand vows as a social matter. I did not enter a void but rather a community of people who each took the same vows and made the same public pledges as I did. By my vows, not only did I enter into a special relationship with the Lord but also I also entered into a special relationship with the Jesuits. Perhaps that's why we are so friendly when we are with one another: we each made the same fundamental life choices.

Years ago I thought that religious vows were not unlike marital ones. But I was mistaken. I never vowed to be with anyone in particular, though I did vow to stay in the Society of Jesus. I am vowed to the constantly changing collective, but to no one in particular. So unlike marriage, there is no other.

As I celebrate nearly forty years as a Jesuit, I am grateful for my vocation, but I wish that I had a constant companion with whom now I could sit down and think about Syracuse, Fordham, Weston, or Rome. Luckily I have my brother and sisters and these friends with whom I hope to remain in friendship for the next thirty years. In fact, if I could trade my siblings and my three friends for a specific constant companion, I wouldn't. The former are simply essential to my life.

I think married couples also have a need for friendship. I have been told time and again that one of the greatest challenges to contemporary marriage is the insistence, not simply that one's spouse is one's best friend, but that there is no need for any other. Many marriages suffer when they withdraw from friends, when they singularly depend upon and place their expectations on the one person to whom they are vowed.

There's an irony here: we religious have plenty of friends but not long-standing best friends, while couples have their best friend but not enough other friends. Yet in both instances, friends are necessary.

Even though the formulas we each express in our particular vows do not refer to friends, still friendship is deeply connected to both forms of vowed life. Vowed life, whether marital or religious, does not remove us from community but rather identifies us within it. Vowed life socializes us and helps us to live for others. Indeed, normally, we cannot live out our promises before God unless there is a network of friends supporting us.

Some of the great theological writing today on marriage, by Lisa Sowle Cahill, Julie Hanlon Rubio, David Matzko McCarthy, and David Cloutier, insist that marriage needs to have a public social ethic. People marry and form families for love, but in that love is a deeper appreciation for the neighbor and the common good.

An interesting contemporary phenomenon is the growing number of single persons who choose this as another form of (vowed) life. They more than married persons and vowed religious know the integral value of friendship. Unlike having a community or a spouse and family, they know that their friendships are essential to the life they live.

Curiously, when we think of vows and promises we think of words that once uttered should never be broken. But I think that in living out those words we err, if we think that the one who uttered them is singularly responsible for her or his pledge. Our pledges were and remain public. The community needs these pledges, and so they in general and friends specifically help us through the decisions we make; and later on, others enter our lives and in no less a way help us in living out our fundamental choices today.

Meaningful words are not uttered to be privately regarded. As human beings, words and language are the way we communicate; that is, the way we enter into communion. By words we signify what we intend. But what we intend, like the words themselves, only come to fruition in our relationship with others.

Chapter Fifteen

Apologizing

Are there words that have a lasting effect? Are there expressions that can change our own personal world? Are there phrases that when we hear them we are deeply affected and inevitably the moment of hearing the phrase becomes, if you will, memorable?

I think that the language of love is almost always effective. Whenever we hear someone say, "I love you," we hear it as something new, terribly important, and resonant with our deeper feelings. We do not forget easily the instances in which the words "I love you" are spoken, and we can recall our own responses to such occasions. Whether those words were welcomed, a surprise, longed for, or expected, generally speaking, "I love you" leaves a lasting impression on us.

Words can deeply affect us. The horrible phrase, "I hate you," even as we read it, is hurtful and disturbing. We do not want to have it said to us and we do not want it said at all. Like love, it is a very effective phrase; it causes in the hearer hurt and pain, which does not easily pass away. The words leave a lasting impression on the recipient, words that are never easily undone. In fact, the words affect the hearer sometimes so much that one's relationships with others become tainted simply because the hate words have had such an impact. Indeed, the intentionality of the speaker of the words generally wishes this harm on the other.

There can be other phrases that affect us. Phrases like "You are my best friend," "I will also be faithful to you," "You make me feel good," "I don't know how I could ever get by without you." These phrases of tenderness and affection stay with us; we remember the context in which they were said and we remember the narrative of the moment.

Likewise, there are harmful phrases, not as harsh as "I hate you," but still alienating and deeply felt words: "I cannot trust you," "You betrayed me," "I think you are a selfish person." Words like these have a lasting effect on us.

Words of Apology

Another phrase that has great possibilities to affect us are the words of apology. Each of us can remember how restorative these words are. Let me highlight this with a story.

While teaching at Weston Jesuit, I became the director of the licentiate program. I wanted it be one of the finest programs in the country. One year, a new licentiate student from overseas arrived who was lively and engaging, quickly liked by his fellow students and faculty. I began to think of him, however, as an "operator." I discovered that he was doing some creative course planning: he was getting credit for two courses, while doing the same work for each. I confronted him on the matter and said he could not do it. He responded by saying that the idea came from a faculty member, who was directing him in his research project. He accepted my position that he was only getting credit for one course. In hindsight, his explanation made perfect sense, but I did not trust him. For his next two years at Weston Jesuit, I kept my eye on him. He certainly knew that I was on the lookout, though he never said anything. For instance, whenever he and I were together in a group, such as meetings for all the licentiate students, he could see my trust and validation of others contrasted by my suspicion of him.

Over the years he has become a priest and a theologian, a very fine one. He is as lively and engaging as the day he arrived at Weston. On one return visit we expressed simple greetings, but after seeing him briefly I began to realize that years ago I had done him wrong.

Last year, he stayed at Boston College for a few weeks to do some writing. Seeing him prompted me to picture what his experience was like during those two years in the licentiate program. I remembered what it was like being an international student, but I did not know how it felt, if your director has it in for you. I began to think of not my side of my actions, but his side of my actions. I was disturbed by what I had done.

I invited him out one evening. After a light conversation, I told him that I asked him out for a particular reason: to acknowledge that I was wrong, that I treated him unfairly, and that I wanted to apologize. I also noted that at the time I was new as the director and wanted to give the program credibility, but I did not need to sacrifice students along the way.

Not only was he relieved that I acknowledged that my assumptions were mistaken and harsh but also he was very moved when I said I was sorry for my disposition toward him and asked him to accept my apology. Strangely, he had always wanted my respect, but I had squandered it for years. Now I was apologizing, and he felt finally welcomed. Subsequently he gave me a book that he had authored, with an inscription of gratitude and promise.

His acceptance of my apology made me feel very good, too. It liberated me from what I had done. I could see too, how fine a person he was by the generosity of his forgiveness. I saw, in the light now of our reconciled conversation, that by not looking at how he was affected by my actions, I remained in my uncritical and judgmental world. Above all I saw more clearly how I had alienated this fine fellow. Still, by his accepting my apology, he helped me put behind myself the regret I had for my actions.

Apologies as Effective

The late German theologian, Franz Böckle, once wrote that until we confess our sins, we do not know them. The act of actually confessing our sins opens us up to understanding better the nature of our sins. Böckle wrote that confessing sins was an effective act; by it we learn much more about our sinfulness.

Similarly, though we may admit to ourselves when we are wrong, when we admit it to the one we have wronged, the act of admission opens to us far greater understanding about the nature of our fault. I have always thought Böckle was right on this. Apologies matter.

Of course, many do not believe this. Some of us are old enough to remember the banality of the movie *Love Story*, and the popular debate it yielded over the words: "Love means never having to say you are sorry." In the aftermath of that discussion, most people realized that lasting love is only possible if apologies, forgiveness, and reconciliation are a part of the relationship.

Apologies matter. I could see in this fellow that by my apology, the long history of my suspicion of him was now lifted. He no longer felt excluded, and even though he knew to trust his own self throughout the ordeal and to think that I was the one who was wrong, still, by my acknowledgment, he was validated in the belief that I was unfair. No one likes misjudgment, and no matter what we tell ourselves about the one who misjudges, we still bear the weight of the other's judgment. When he heard me apologize, the history of my poor treatment of him came to an end for him and for me.

Two years ago when I realized that I had been wrong to him, I could have let it go and just been friendly toward him. He would have welcomed the change but with some hesitancy. The same unease that was between us would inevitably remain because the experience of years ago needed to be acknowledged. My words of apology allowed me to see what I had done but also allowed him to know more clearly that it was my fault, not his. The words freed us both; we are friends today.

"I'm sorry," "It was my fault," "I regret the harm I caused you." These words liberate the oppressor and the oppressed. We saw their effectiveness when Pope Benedict aboard a plane to the United States acknowledged his fault and those of his brothers in the sex abuse scandal. When he later met with the victims, I am sure both sides were affected. The words having been spoken and the guilt being acknowledged opened up the history of sin to new possibilities.

When the Australian government apologized to the Aborigines of the continent, everyone was affected, but especially the Aborigines. They were being liberated from a long history of harsh judgment, and their narratives were now being validated by those who for long periods of time thought otherwise.

We are very limited people, all too human. The act of apologizing is hardly a humiliating action, though many fear it is. It rather restores balances, removes harm, and offers hope. Apologies matter to the one who offers them and to the one who receives them.

Chapter Sixteen

APPRECIATING THE
LIMITS OF LANGUAGE

My dad used to say, "A written word can always be erased, but a spoken one can never be retracted." He used it on many occasions, at home and at work, among family, friends, neighbors, and colleagues. Whenever someone regretted something said rashly, my dad would cite his proverb. Few things were predictable about my dad, but whenever anyone said, "Boy, I wish I hadn't said that," my dad was ready to share his lesson within five seconds of the penitent's confession.

As I get older, I realize it is a pretty good lesson to keep in mind. Many times I stopped myself from saying something that I really wanted to say but kept telling myself, "You're going to regret this. You'll never be able to retract it."

Still sometimes we let it rip, and it is not just that what we said cannot be taken back, but the harm that accompanied it cannot be undone. We may have said something stupid, unkind, unthinking in the heat of anger or resentfulness. Words came out of our mouths that should have remained unspoken. We jeopardized a relationship that matters a great deal. When we said what we said, words flowed.

When we try to take back what we said, we are often at a loss for words. We accused, judged, or ridiculed another with rhetorical finesse, but when we try to undo what has been done, words fail us.

Explanations are fine, so long as they come with an apology. We learned the effect of an apology as children because parents teach their children to apologize many times over. We learned that a simple "I'm sorry" is usually fairly effective.

Often we want to avoid making an apology; we want instead to simply "explain." These explanations are usually lame; the words we use are often void and shallow. Until we take ownership for what we did and apologize, the explanation is really not effective. In these instances, we encounter the limits of language—as we begin to offer a reason for our lamentable conduct, we usually discover, right in the middle of our attempts, that our offer just does not do it. Our lame explanation is nothing more than a poor excuse. Held hostage by the limits of our words, we capitulate and say, "I'm sorry."

STORIES OF HUMOR AND SUFFERING

Whenever we aim to entertain by story, we find easily the words that we want. When we tell a comic story, we add all sorts of accessories and make the act of telling it longer and the hearing of it even more worthwhile. The funnier the story is, the lengthier it becomes, and the more we add all sorts of ironic insights along the way. The story may not be true, but that is beside the point.

Like humorous stories, the narratives of gossip, the purported account of what a third party said or did, look for an audience as well. In these accounts, language becomes a constructive tool to amuse others, at another's expense. We add more and more particulars to our revelations and as we continue our claims, we find we talk easily and are hardly at a lack for words. When it comes to gossip, the devil is indeed in the details. And God knows we can generate enough of them.

Often, when we want to tell more serious stories, especially those of sorrow, suffering, or grief, our entire way of telling the account is different. A sad story moves at a much slower pace, with plenty of pauses, and each word becomes weightier as we proceed. We do not want to compromise the integrity of the account; we are as exacting in our telling as the evident sadness that exudes from the story. A narrative of sadness generally has an economy to it, which comic tales do not have. When the account is regretful, tragic, or pathetic, our words are more carefully chosen and the story itself is starker.

Sharing sadness and pain and suffering is not an easy task, and language often does not make it any easier. As we encounter the limits of life or human happiness, we often encounter frustration in the limits of language. As we experience loss, we are often slow and sometimes even unable to express the suffering. And when we want to respond to human suffering we often believe (rightly?) that words might demean the story we just heard. The catch-22 of human life is that often words fail us when we are most in need of them.

Probably the most apparent gulf between experience and language occurs when we are in pain. Ironically, despite this connection, the body in pain is often unable to express itself. Paul Brand captures in *In His Image* this phenomenon by considering chronic pain and its inability to free the body to speak. Brand offers some resolution by highlighting the empathetic quality of pain and by demonstrating that the witness to one in pain can sometimes communicate, validate, acknowledge, and even articulate the depth of the pain.

Other writers suggest that the witness to another's pain ought to become aware of his or her own narratives of pain so as to resonate empathetically with the one in pain. Still others see in the psalms a vehicle for expressing pain. In reading aloud the psalms of lament by the bedside of one in pain, we can express solidarity with another and with our lament ask God, "Where are you?" and "Where is the relief?"

When we are alone in pain, the very thing we want to do is express it, but sometimes, we can only utter cries, shouts, and moans. We become illiterate in our pain, and even the act of praying is itself fraught with challenge. St. Paul in Romans 8:23–27 acknowledges the experience of pain but tells us that the Holy Spirit can come to our aid and express what we long to say. Rather than urging us to silence and resignation, he sees the Spirit as being able to express the depths of our pain.

> We know that all creation is groaning in labor pains even until now; and not only that, but we ourselves, who have the first fruits of the Spirit, we also groan within ourselves as we wait for adoption, the redemption of our bodies.
>
> For in hope we were saved. Now hope that sees for itself is not hope. For who hopes for what one sees?
>
> But if we hope for what we do not see, we wait with endurance.
>
> In the same way, the Spirit too comes to the aid of our weakness; for we do not know how to pray as we ought, but the Spirit itself intercedes with inexpressible groanings.
>
> And the one who searches hearts knows what is the intention of the Spirit, because it intercedes for the holy ones according to God's will.

MEMORY AND LOSS

In stories of sorrow, we want to remember the details. We try to hold on to a part of our history that though lost, now lives in our memories. Our memory is very affective, but often it is not terribly effective. It does not retain everything it once witnessed and cannot remember what it has already forgotten. In fact, it does not even recognize what it has not remembered. We tell a tale that may actually be considerably mistaken, but unless another witness challenges our account, we remain unknowingly as the teller of the tale that never happened.

Still, other times our memory may not fully serve us, and we know it. On those occasions, if the narrative is entertaining, we do not mind making something up along the way. If they are stories of sorrow, we mourn the details lost.

It is hard not to find the words and details of a story long ago lived out. For memory, the Italians use the word *ricordare*, "to bring back to the heart," but sometimes what we bring back is not all that accurate. Listen, for instance, to someone telling a story from an event that you shared with the narrator. Have you ever walked away from hearing it told, only to say to yourself, "That is not how I remember it"?

PLANS AND IMAGINATION

Language has a deep orientation to the future. We make promises and pledges and think and dream of what may be. When we think of tomorrow, we hope for something better, and through language we entertain many of the possibilities that lay ahead. Let us go out for dinner, let us take a trip, let us go shopping, etc. Making plans often generates a positive stance of friendship, solidarity, and fellowship, and words are helpful tools toward realizing them.

With family or friends, we allow our imagination to take over, making our hopes specific, attainable, and tangible. When we plan for the future, our language is pregnant with thick and ready expectations.

Imagining the future prompts us to find the words that embody our dreams. That might be a struggle, but often enough we find them. Interestingly, when we are not beset by challenges or feeling loss, when instead we are happy, hopeful, or just plain chatty, the words come. It is as if, in moments of sadness, language knows enough to stand outside the door of the inner self, giving it time to get its bearings; when there is joy, however, the words are easily found and spoken.

LISTENING AND RESPONDING

Listening to narratives of humor or achievement is easy and enjoyable. Listening to those of pain, betrayal, grief, or loss is a challenge for each of us. We are often awkward as we try to attend to each word being spoken, while thinking at the same time, "How will I possibly respond?" The listening alone requires considerable skill, but finding the right words is truly daunting. "I know how you feel" may seem to the sufferer terribly dismissive; "don't worry" may provoke a resentful silence or an angry string of words. Sometimes we admit, however, "I don't know what to say," "I'm at a loss for words," "I'm speechless." These phrases actually can help both of us understand the sometimes limited ways we honor one another.

Sometimes, however, the teller of the narrative has to give the listener a sign of what they want and need to hear. I have learned this recently. Often when a friend or colleague asked me how I was, I would say "fine." Fine? Since September 2008 when I was discovered to have a stage III melanoma, I have had two surgeries, a month of daily infusions, and then eleven months of taking injections of interferon three times a week. The side effects of the interferon are considerable: fevers, shakes, hives, nausea, fatigue, etc. Still, having lost fifteen pounds and having great color, I actually look better than I did before September! Since no one sees the stocking compressing my leg, the eczema all over me, or the nightly sweats, I look as "fine" as I say I am.

A wise friend heard me responding to a colleague's concern about my health. Later my friend stopped me, "You know, you're going to be completely well, but not until you finish the treatment. Why do you say 'fine'? If you want people to ask you something more specific or offer something consoling, you have to give them an opening."

"What should I say?"

"When they ask you how you are, don't say fine, say 'I'm OK.' The modesty and ambiguity of it conveys, I think, exactly how you are. But don't walk away after you say 'OK.' From there on in, it is up to them."

Language has its limits, but it has its meanings, too, and sometimes that meaning is found when we replace "fine" with an "OK." From phrases as simple as "OK," "I'm sorry," "I'm at a loss for words," we can communicate a whole range of honest insight because language, like knowledge, has its limits, and the humanity of acknowledging those limits makes our words and our awkward conversations honest and promising.

Chapter Seventeen

REPORTING THE TRUTH
TO HURT ANOTHER

I have been reading a big, wonderful book, *A Code of Jewish Ethics, Volume 1: You Shall Be Holy* by Rabbi Joseph Telushkin. This is the first of a three-volume work and deals primarily with character development. The second volume, *Love Your Neighbor*, will address the ethics pertinent to interpersonal relations: obligations to the weakest and most vulnerable; between employers and employees; between Jews and non-Jews; between those who disagree; etc. The final volume, not yet named, will deal with family, friendship, and community.

"THE EVIL TONGUE"

Telushkin has a wonderful style and takes the reader through a variety of virtues and vices in this volume, but then toward the end of it, he develops a special section dedicated to fair speech and introduces us to the evil tongue, *lashon hara*. Telushkin describes it as "true statements that harm, embarrass, cause financial damage to, or lower the status of the person being discussed." Another rabbi calls it "mean-spirited truth."

In any event, this is such an ordinary, frequently expressed vice that we sometimes underestimate its pervasiveness. Moreover, as ordinary as it is it still has a sophistication about it that makes the hearer of the evil tongue seem innocent!

The issue is not whether a statement is true; the question is whether passing on the information to another is fair. A perfect example is when a person in a moment of frustration expresses an unkind comment about a relative and the hearer believes that the relative *should* know about it and informs the relative. The informer acted on the assumption that he or she had to tell the relative; the relative needed to know. Telushkin notes that not surprisingly most family feuds are started by *lashon hara*. Someone tells a relative something that the relative was never meant to hear. As one philosopher noted, "I lay down as a fact that if all men knew what others say of them, there would not be four friends left in the world."

It is the self-righteousness of the informer that motivates the informer to tell the truth to hurt another. The moral superiority of the informer drives her or him to repeat what does not bear repeating. Of course, this form of conduct is commonplace and fairly harmful and is practiced with sanctimonious license. Telushkin writes, "*lashon hara* is a gratuitous act of wrongdoing."

The rabbi points out that one of the great evils of *lashon hara* is that since it does not happen in the victim's presence, the victim cannot defend herself or himself against the vicious one. Worse, unlike a physical injury that happens in one moment, often a repeated comment gets repeated again and again, causing an ever-expanding circle of harm, all in the so-called interest in truth.

Recognizing that we all practice *lashon hara* more than we care to admit, Jewish law actually differentiates between those who occasionally speak it and those who are habitual speakers of it. The latter are perpetual threats to family and communal life. They bring upheaval to all who live in the world of presumed trusting relations that we need to have with one another.

Because the goal of *lashon hara* is to undermine another's reputation and authority, the Jewish tradition particularly warns against practicing *lashon hara* against rabbis. This is not solely to protect the rabbi; rather, *lashon hara* inevitably diminishes a rabbi's ability to do good and to serve the community. It robs the rabbi and the community. As we shall see, other communities of faith have the same threat.

"Clergy Killers"

I have already referred to the collection of essays that Joseph Kotva and I edited, *Practice What You Preach: Virtues, Ethics and Power in the Lives of Pastoral Ministers and Their Congregations.* Therein was an essay by Paul Wadell, and it was precisely on this very issue. He looked at those who told the truth about a pastor precisely to hurt the pastor and to undermine her or his authority. He used a very striking term to describe those who practiced this *lashon hara* against their pastor: he called them "clergy killers."

He described the case of a pastor who finds herself not able to name how or why her authority has been so diminished. Wadell writes:

> Suggestive questions are raised "with the best of intentions and the good of the church in mind." The pastor senses something is not right, but is unsure what it might be. She no longer feels quite as welcome in parish gatherings. She notices conversations shift when she enters a room. She sees people who once received her warmly now turning away to avoid her.

Lashon hara isolates the victim, leaving the victim with no options. The victim is, as the phrase goes, out of the loop, and the strategy of *lashon hara* is precisely to keep the victim out of the loop. This is incredibly sinister because someone is saying something truthful about someone who has no idea of this form of reporting.

In institutions of faith, we sometimes sanction this practice institutionally. Wadell, for instance, continues his report about the pastor, noting how the clergy killers are actually protected. He writes that when the pastor "asks about the specific accusations and tries to confront her accusers, she is told that confidentiality must be maintained." This struck me as a particularly "Christian Moment." One can get denounced without knowing by whom. In organizations with high vertical organizations, often enough those who practice *lashon hara* get protected. They serve a function. . . .

With reason, the great Jewish philosopher Maimonides called the one who practiced *lashon hara* "a spy."

In the Society of Jesus we have a very dated, and I think ethically problematic, format for evaluating periodically a man in formation. With the unhappy title of *informationes*, these are forms with ten questions that basically ask the informant to write out his assessment of a man, according to how he lives his vows, works with others, recreates, etc. Some provinces use them two times before a man takes final vows. Other provinces use them as often as five or six times.

While many informants fill out these forms with generosity and truthfulness, there is no training on how to fill this out nor is there any accountability for the informant. A person can report hearsay or practice *lason hara* and a provincial has to figure out whether the reports are accurate and fair. Often the candidate does not see the reports, does not know who made the reports, and is not given any extensive information as to what they contained. They are highly fallible instruments that encourage reporting. Without any ethical guidelines for them, they are, I think, a threat to the individual as well as the life of the community. (Keenan, "Are Informationes Ethical?" *Studies in the Spirituality of Jesuits* 29, September 1997)

WHAT ABOUT REAL THREATS TO THE COMMUNITY?

Certainly you may ask, "But after the sexual abuse scandal, shouldn't we be vigilant about what our leadership does? Weren't we too deferential to clergy and bishops?" There's some truth in these questions. For instance, many presumed not to believe reports about priests molesting children. Many presumed that bishops once informed would act to protect the children. But the sexual abuse of vulnerable people is so clearly an issue of injustice that it shouldn't be discussed, it should be reported immediately! The problem in the sexual abuse scandal wasn't that there was *lashon hara*; the problem was that when parents and others made actual reports they were ignored, ridiculed, or rejected outright. Discussion wasn't the issue, reporting was.

Thomas Aquinas raised the question of when we should report a person's wrongdoing. He called it, as did everyone else, fraternal correction. In the *Summa theologiae* (II.II.33) he distinguished two reasons to correct another: when one's conduct is actually hurting another, and this is when we act for justice, and when someone is actually hurting their relationship with God by their conduct, and this is when we act for charity. In both instances, we are to be virtuous in the correction. I correct my neighbor because I want her or him to stop hurting another (justice) or because he or she is hurting themselves (charity).

Unlike the *informationes* or other acts of *lashon hara*, in each case, I am not talking about them, I am talking to them. And, if it is a case where they will not hear my correction and they are hurting another, then I must report them to the proper authorities. But the entire context of the correction is in the context of transparency and honesty.

These serious issues are not the matter of *lashon hara*. *Lashon hara* is fairly frivolous; no one's good is at stake except the one whose "truth" we are discussing, and her or his reputation is precisely what we are seeking to undermine. Virtues, and especially charity and justice, have little role here. Moreover, we are not directly speaking to the person whose reputation we are savaging. In fraternal correction we tell the person whose conduct is wrong that they are wrong; we don't discuss it with others.

Combating Our Evil Tongues

For the most part *lashon hara* names the very smug practice of trash-ing a person but under the warrant that we are telling the truth. Both Telushkin and Wadell make clear to us that it is, unfortunately, a common action. Telushkin offers us constructive remedies, the first being that we begin to learn how frequently we practice it. With com-plete rabbinical common sense, he offers this advice:

> Choose one day, perhaps the first day of each month, as a Speak No Evil Day. For twenty-four hours, guard your tongue from saying anything negative about or to anyone. And, on the other days of the month, choose a two hour period each day when you will be particularly careful to speak no *lashon hara*. Some people agree to do this, then jokingly resolve to carry out their commitment between 3:00 and 5:00 a.m. It is best to schedule the two hours during a period that includes a meal, for this is when many of us are likely to speak *lashon hara*.

He adds, "If the above seems too demanding, try this: Over the coming week, make sure that at least once a day you resist saying a negative truth about someone." Not bad advice, if you ask me.

Chapter Eighteen

Lying and the Obligation
to Get the Story Right

On August 13, 2004, the American chef of French cuisine, Julia
Child, died. The next day National Public Radio rebroadcasted an
interview with her in 2003.

The interview was, not surprisingly, interesting, engaging,
and witty. In the middle of it, Child commented, "I never dropped
a chicken." The reference was to a very comical, nearly mythic narrative that eventually appeared as a skit on *Saturday Night Live.* The
story went like this: while preparing a dinner on television from her
legendary kitchen, Child dropped a partially cooked chicken on the
floor, dusted it off, tossed it back into the pan, and commented, "Remember, you are alone in the kitchen, and no one can see you."

During the interview she tried rectifying the account: It was a
simple potato pancake that fell onto the work table when she tried to
flip it. She put it back in the pan, pressed it back into shape, and said,
"Remember, you are alone in the kitchen, and no one can see you."

A few days after she died, I was sitting at breakfast with a
seventy-five-year-old Jesuit who commented on the death of Julia
Child and added, "You know whenever I think of Julia Child, I think

of the time she dropped the chicken . . . ." After breakfast, I went online to Google, "Julia Child dropped chicken." Astonishingly, I found 1,750 sites. No matter her efforts, most people like my Jesuit friend remember Child for one thing that she never did, tossing food from the floor into her dinner.

As funny as the story was, the interview was poignant: America's most famous chef was defending herself self-effacingly against the claim that she cooked from the floor. Certainly the story that she would and did do something like that contradicts the very stuff of her legacy. Still, her predicament was well captured by a contemporary of hers. As president John F. Kennedy noted: "The great enemy of the truth is very often not the lie—deliberate, contrived and dishonest—but the myth—persistent, persuasive and unrealistic."

FALSIFYING NARRATIVES

I find the story a good example of how the easy change in details falsifies an entire narrative. Replace a detail and you have a new story. Who changed the potato to a chicken or the table top to the floor? Who gave the first account? Who reported seeing Child on TV drop a chicken on the floor, pick it up, dust it off, and toss it into a pot? And, how many (thousands?) claimed they saw the episode and validated the false account? How easily do we get the details wrong?

In the 2008 presidential race, we had multitudinous reports on shifting details in daily narratives. One of the most spectacular was the recurring claim that Senator Barack Obama is a Muslim. Of course, this one, like most others, has no source. There's always a certain anonymity to these stories.

As in a presidential race, it seems, in parishes mythic rumors are commonplace. Sometimes they are genuinely funny, like the Child story, though often, someone pays for it, as did Child. Other rumors are more deliberately vicious, as in the Obama claim.

The narratives in a parish have of course an element of truth in them. Like Child who did after all toss a pancake, the parish narrative begins with something possible, even probable (at least to the listener). The element of truth gives it its credibility, for a falsehood only has credibility if it has that ring of truth to it.

Of course, these narratives are all lies. Truth telling usually occurs in a narrative; truth telling is really about getting the narrative right. Exaggeration is bending it somewhat, and lying is altering the narrative's purpose. Often it's hard to distinguish when an exaggeration makes the narrative a lie.

Lying and the Moral Tradition

Lying is an interesting phenomenon. It is one practice that differentiates God from us: God cannot, after all, lie; we can. The writer of the Letter to the Hebrews (6:13–18; see also Num. 23:19, Ps. 89:35) tells us that, unlike ourselves, it is impossible for God to lie. Lying, unfortunately, belongs to the human and also to the devil, whom Jesus refers to as the Father of lies (John 8:44).

From the beginning of the Scriptures, lying is prohibited, as in the two accounts of the Decalogue (Ex. 2:16; Deut. 5:20). God abhors deceitful persons and destroys those who lie (Ps. 5:6; Prov. 6:16–19), warns us against taking refuge in lying (Isaiah 28:15), and so forbids lying to one another (Lev. 19:11), a command that Paul reiterates in his letter to the Colossians (3:9).

Like the Scriptures, the moral tradition has always judged lying to be wrong. Aristotle held that lying was never right, and in the Christian tradition Augustine and Aquinas each argued that lying was always a sin.

In his discussion on lying in the *Summa Theologiae*, Thomas Aquinas writes that the "essential notion of a lie" is found when "a person intends to say what is false." Thomas goes on to say that the lie is not first and foremost the intention to deceive but rather the simple act of intending to speak a falsehood.

Thomas makes lying easy. Whenever we exaggerate, shift attribution, change context, or alter details, we lie. To the claim that we meant no harm, Thomas gives no hearing. A lie is the intention to not tell the truth.

Here we see that Thomas is also imposing a burden on us: we have an obligation to tell the story as it is. We cannot bypass the truth but rather are obliged to witness to it; we cannot change the facts, bend the truth, or spruce things up. We have to tell the truth.

GETTING NARRATIVES RIGHT

We know that there are people to whom we do not give the benefit of the doubt, people of whom we are not inclined to speak well. Precisely, concerning these people we should be most suspicious of our own ability to give a truthful narrative. We need a healthy self-doubt of our own motives to distort accounts pertaining to people whom we do not find credible. Thus we must be vigilant of our own attempt to cast a narrative involving such people. Our inclination to distort is extraordinary, and therefore we must beware of the details whenever we tell narratives about those whom we avoid, dislike, or distrust.

Journalists have a particular responsibility here. They need to make sure that they report accurately. But like us, they need to attend to their biases, as well. Journalists who suspect the truth claims of others must in turn suspect their own ability to depict fairly the persons they suspect.

We live with such irresponsible forms of discourse around us that there must be a greater accountability to the truth. We live in a world where attribution so often misses the mark and the specificity of a person's belief on a particular matter is reduced, dismissed, or discarded.

Ironically many misrepresentations are made in the name of ethics. Often, we find that people are accused of positions they never took, but because they spoke positively on an issue, they are attributed with much more extreme stances than they actually took. This is nothing more than crude consequentialism. Perhaps some believe that they have the right to distort the truth of another's position because the other has taken a stand with which they disagree. But there is no merit to this presupposition. While nothing is won by distorting another's position, still in many debates about ethics, truthful reporting is often the first fatality.

Preachers, pastors, and their assistants can help here. I know from my own experience that preachers, pastors, and their assistants can fan untruths and make gross exaggerations. But they undermine their own claims when they do this. How can we preach the Gospel if we don't witness to the truth? How can we ask for honest accountability from our own congregations if we are not witnessing to the details of our opponents with care and concern?

Augustine and Thomas rightly feared that lying corrupts human nature and human discourse. Human discourse depends on the good faith of others. Sometimes in order to maintain that good faith we need to go against our own tendencies. But, we can only do that in the service of truth.

Both of them, as theologians, see in Jesus the Word made flesh and in the symbol of the Word the reason to tell the truth. If the entire communication of God in revelation to humanity is through the lens of truth, why in the name of God would we compromise the truth? To lie is an offense to the Incarnation itself; to lie is to falsify the possibility of what God wants us to understand. Truth is the very foundation by which we live in trust with one another. If the truth erodes, the trust does as well; but, if the trust erodes, the truth can too. Inevitably truth precedes trust; inevitably the only way we can move forward in trust is in truth.

We know from experience, whatever the case, that lying diminishes trust and credibility. But we know that the foundations that lies destroy are the very foundations that truth builds up.

Part IV

WORDS

Chapter Nineteen

Beautiful Words, Good Words

As an undergraduate at Fordham, I went to see Julie Harris in the *Belle of Amherst*. The terrific one-woman show captured brilliantly one of America's greatest poets, Emily Dickinson, a woman who was very much in her own home and her own world.

Throughout the play, Dickinson is on the lookout for wonderful words. She notes them down in a pad that she carries with her. If she hears or thinks of a word that expresses its own power and purpose, she writes it down. "Now that's a good word," she often says.

For Dickinson, one word could trigger a poem. For each of us, words can prompt memories, images, or insights.

I learned a lot more about words when I taught English to eleventh grade boys at Canisius High School in Buffalo. There I had the privilege of working with a fellow Jesuit, Paul Naumann, a brilliant teacher and great advisor.

Most of our classes were divided between writing composition and reading great literature. In the latter, we always included a play by Shakespeare, which we read line by line. For the juniors it was *Antony and Cleopatra*.

We also called on the students each day to recite poetry from memory. This exercise was to help them internalize poetry by learning each poem "by heart." At the beginning of every class I would call on several students to recite the lines from the assigned poem, and afterward I would write the next two lines of the poem on the blackboard for the following day's exercises. Needless to say, the students liked briefer poems.

Naumann was frustrated with the way they recited. There was nothing from the heart in their recitation. They appreciated nothing of the beauty of the poem, or for that matter, its words. In fact, they seemed to just string the words together, without any appreciation for why the poet wrote in the first place. Since they were just repeating words, Naumann arrived in his class one day and wrote in Latin the opening lines from the *Aeneid*. Each morning for two weeks he added the next two lines. The students were astonished, with many pleading that they knew no Latin. "Too bad. You were only memorizing words. You didn't memorize the English poems. What does it matter if it is in English or Latin? By the way, if next week I give you an English poem and you recite it that way you have been, you'll be reciting Greek the rest of the semester." Their skills in recitation improved dramatically.

A VARIETY OF GOOD WORDS

I learned from Naumann as I had from *The Belle of Amherst* the beauty, power, and purpose of words. I learned how words work. Uttering a word with only six or seven letters can unleash a variety of memories or expectations and can lead a listener to a new place or an old one. We can hear a particular word and somehow it immediately evokes an image: the one word captures a whole entire picture. Think of the word *trickle*—can't you see it? There it is, the water trickling down from a leaf or from someone's back. Now as Dickinson would say, "Trickle is a good word."

I mentioned this to a Jesuit here who just defended his doctoral dissertation in philosophy. A native of Chad, he asked what was I writing. I told him. "Give me a word." I said, "Trickle," and he extended his right arm above his head and with his fingers imitated in a downward motion the movement of *trickle*.

Some of these words are very effective. They quickly prompt us to conjure up images. *Plunge*—now that's a word with a wide array of images. We can think of the stock market on some bad days last year. "Plunge," you say? "Tanked" is more like it. But we can also plunge into the ocean or the pool. More robust than jump or dive, plunge is about a quick and total immersion; it goes deep and is often shocking, like a plunging neckline, plunging a knife into someone, or taking the plunge oneself.

Some words do not evoke pictures but sounds. Words like *quack, bark, moo, meow*, and *chirp* have very specific references. *Quack* makes us think not of any animal, but only ducks. Quack not only prompts us to imagine a billed, web-footed, white-bellied, down-feathered waddling animal, it also helps us to hear it. Just imagine a group of kindergarten children taught the word *quack*. Listen to the crowd of them imitating ducks. They love to make noise, but they love imitation as well. Quack and you're a duck; bark and you are a dog.

Other words are about human communication. *Giggle*, can you hear it? There's something childlike, playful, and innocent about giggling, no? Doesn't a giggle make you smile? Or doesn't *whisper* make you strain to hear those words being uttered, softly yet closely from one's lips to another's ear? *Sigh* conveys a whole spectrum, eliciting sometimes sympathy, other times consternation, but in every instance we hear that breath leaving tiredly another's own body.

Titles and categories convey a great deal: you hear *Chick flix* and you think *Beaches* or the Lifetime channel. I hear *talk radio* and a chill goes down my spine. And the word *melodrama* in a movie review is just about as damnable a word as one can get.

Finally, some words are so simple in their beauty that they are unparalleled in significance. While embracing their simplicity, we can nonetheless write volumes on their meaning. Just meditate on the word *love*. Or consider another: the nineteenth-century senator

Chauncey Depew, when he was ninety-two, was asked: "What is the most beautiful word in the language?" The elderly lawyer quickly replied: "Home."

JESUS, THE GOOD WORD

The early church knew the power of words, especially as they sought to express their understanding of Jesus of Nazareth. The great struggle of the early church leaders was trying to understand the divinity and the humanity of Jesus. Rather than making the concepts mutually exclusive, the early leaders put them together. We may have understood who he was, but then what should Jesus be called? Messiah?

The ignominious death of Jesus made the question all the more challenging. How could Jesus be Messiah if he died on a cross? The death of Jesus became such a stumbling block that he became known as the stumbling block (a wonderfully suggestive phrase). The stumbling block is precisely the Messiah.

Despite an array of titles and references, three other titles are especially significant. "Son of God" captures an entire relationship between God and humanity in Jesus Christ. In the epiphanies, in the river Jordan or the Transfiguration, the witness to Jesus is God who calls him Son. Others do the same: Nathanael calls Jesus the Son of God (John 1:49) and Peter confesses that Jesus is the Christ, the Son of God. (Mt. 16:15–16). Clearly, Son of God refers to the divine intimacy between Jesus and God.

"Son of Man" is the title Jesus uses for himself, repeatedly, more than eighty times. No one else uses it but Stephen, and then as he dies seeing as a vision of the great eschatological delivery (Acts 7:55). Though the title refers to the vision of *The Book of Daniel* (7:13), Jesus seems to use it to refer to the fullness of his own humanity.

The titles Son of God and Son of Man are like the divinity and humanity of Christ. In themselves they are insufficient; together they express Jesus Christ.

No word is more beautiful than *Lord*, because that one word captures all of our hopes. Derived from the Hebrew title for God, *Adonai*, in the Christian Bible it often refers to the effective glory of Jesus Christ. The title appears most often at Easter time: After hearing the command of Jesus to cast the nets off the right side, John informs Peter, "It is the Lord." (John 21:7). After Peter arrives on the shore and Jesus asks Peter three times, "Do you love me?," each time Peter says, "Lord, you know that I love you." And, it is the witness of Thomas, "My Lord and my God" (John 20:28). Even when not explicitly tied to the resurrection, the use of the title is hard to separate from salvation: the Lord saves. As they are fearful of perishing during the storm on the sea, the disciples cry out: "Lord, save us" (MT 8:25).

The salutations in the beginning of the New Testament epistles often start with Paul's greeting in the Lord Jesus Christ (1 Timothy 1:2; Romans 1:3), marking our fellowship with one another. The hymn of Philippians (2:6) celebrates that "Jesus Christ is Lord!" Paul's entire hope and confidence is in the Lord Jesus Christ (Phil. 2:15, 16; Rom 8:10). He considers everything as a loss "because of the supreme good of knowing Christ Jesus my Lord" (Phil. 3:8). In sum, in the Lord we are saved, find our hope, and are friends with one another.

Like the words *love* and *home*, Lord is beautiful because it embodies the horizon of all our expectations. In fact, it is by the Lord that we find our home and live in love. It is by the Lord that each and all of us are called to be holy, "with all those everywhere who call upon the name of our Lord Jesus Christ" (1 Cor. 1:2).

Words of Death and Gratitude

My Mom

My mom, Dolores Keenan, developed a nasty, lingering cold in early November of 2005. About a week later she had a bad fall in her condo. After a week of pain she went to a nearby walk-in clinic, was told that she pulled some back muscles, and received some prescriptions for pain relief.

At the same time, she was set on having two rooms and her staircase re-carpeted and intrepid as ever, she set about moving furniture despite her health.

On the twenty-sixth of November, she began having shortness of breath. I was in Amsterdam lecturing. I called her, was it the pain medication? What was the shortness of breath about? I asked her to call her own doctor.

On the morning of the 30th, she sounded awful, yet she was going to the store to sign the contract so that the carpet could be installed that day. "Should you be driving, Mom? What about calling your physician as well?" "If I don't do it now, I'll have to wait a week. I'm fine."

As I returned to the States on December 1st, my mom admitted herself to Boca Raton community hospital. I called to tell her I would be down by the 3rd.

Aside from a narrow plastic tube strapped under her nose to give her oxygen, she looked great. My mom was an extraordinarily beautiful woman with a compelling elegance. As I arrived, a pulmonary doctor and a cardiologist were seeing her and she seemed in good hands. She was delighted that I had come down.

My brother Sean who lives in nearby West Boca came by to see her and then to take me out to lunch. At lunch I called to see how she was. Her heart rate was erratic. I rushed back to the hospital. "Your mom is going to intensive care."

She felt more secure there; they stabilized her heart rate and began a series of tests. They discovered that Mom broke her back in the fall but they could not repair that until they knew why she wasn't adequately breathing.

My sisters Deb and Jeannine decided to come to Florida and let me return to teaching. They each stayed four days with her. On the 13th, her friend John flew down. He would stay until the 21st when I would return for a Christmas visit. Hopefully by then she would be home. We little realized then that we were each being blessed with our last time alone with Mom.

WORDS

Before I left on December 6th, I faced the prospect that Mom's health was suddenly precarious. Mom knew my love for her, but I wanted to tell her how proud I was of her. I wanted to thank her for teaching me to be ambitious about life. She taught me that by teaching me her own ambition. She was happy to hear what I had to say.

By December 17th, she was much more dependent on oxygen. The doctors transferred her to Miami's major heart and lung facility at the Baptist. Her friend John accompanied her. The doctors there discovered her problem. There was a shunt, some passage that was allowing her deoxygenated blood to mingle with her oxygenated blood. Where was the shunt?

On the 21st I returned and my mom looked as great as always, but now she was receiving fifteen liters of oxygen at 100 percent. She was annoyed because she didn't think she'd be home for Christmas.

Where was the shunt? The physicians had ruled out all other organs but her lungs and heart. The shunt had to be there. On the 22nd they did a bubble angiogram. Her ashen cardiologist was speaking with her. "You are a very sick woman, Dolores, we need to find this shunt." Two invasive tests were prescribed; the less problematic was a pulmonary angiogram.

That night my mom cried for the first time. She telephoned Jeannine, "I don't think I'm leaving this place." She repeated her fear to me. "Mom, I don't know but it's certainly frightening." "At least, with the new carpet, you'll get a good price for the house." My mom, the realist. We laughed.

Her primary physician came in, Stephen Fein. "Dolores, I know that the cardiologist scared you, but I don't think you are that sick. We're going to find this shunt and fix it." He elaborated, and we felt assured; she would be having the pulmonary angiogram early the next morning.

That night Deb called Mom to tell her that Megan (Deb's firstborn who died at nineteen from leukemia) would watch over her during the angiogram.

I arrived at 6:30 the next morning and found Mom praying to the Sacred Heart. Then I accompanied her for the angiogram. We waited for more than an hour and a half. The physician arrived. "Dolores, today we find the shunt and take care of it, Monday we finally fix your back." We felt assured. Just before they came to take Mom in, Deb called. "I know Megan is with you." I added, "Bob is too." (Bob was my brother who died at twenty-six.) "That's good, I can never find Bob." I blessed her, said, "You look great, you'll do fine." She waved.

THE VIGIL

They told me to go to the waiting room and that the physician would see me within an hour or two. Finally they would find something. I was completely at rest and very much sensed that my brother and niece were with Mom and with me. I felt immeasurably assured. I even began thinking about a cruise that I was taking her on in June. It was a very consoling prayer, gentle and affirming . . . all would be well.

After two hours, Mom's sister called, then John, then Jean. I said no one had come in yet. "Maybe they found the shunt and were repairing it," I suggested. Another ninety minutes passed. Then they came to take me into a room where her pulmonary doctor was with a priest. "Oh no," I said. "At the end of the procedure, your mom's heart stopped. It took them twenty-one minutes to get a pulse back. She's been unconscious since the procedure began." I asked them to assure me that they would do everything possible for the next few hours, and then I broke down.

My brother Sean walked in as I was sobbing. Jean called me right then. I told her. I called Deb, my cousin Michael, and Mom's friend John. I told them all to come down as soon as possible. Deb arrived first the next morning, Christmas Eve, at 2 a.m. Then John at 10 a.m., Michael at 12, and finally Jean at 6. Together on Christmas Eve, with Mom intubated on a ventilator.

Deb said to her, "Well, Mom, you certainly figured out a way to get us all together for Christmas."

We had been in this situation before. More recently for Megan, and earlier for Dad. We kept assuring Mom that we were with her and to relax and that she was in good hands. We held her hands, stroked her faced, kissed her, prayed (often the Hail Mary), and continually blessed her. We told her we would be with her through the entire ordeal and that we would care for her as she did for us.

We were very clear and assuring in our words, prayers, and blessings. Whenever a doctor entered the room and start telling us about her brain damage, we would invite him to leave the room with us and continue the conversation outside. No one would talk about her as if she was not there.

Mom was adamant about not wanting life support and, above all, no vents. She had filed three living wills. Now unconsciously she was biting on the tube and using her tongue to push it out of her mouth. A doctor said, "We know your mom is not cognitive; we tell her to stop chewing on the tube, but she does not." We looked around at one another. Clearly the doctors did not know Mom. We assured her that she would soon enough be free.

Stephen Fein told us that seventy-two hours would be more than enough time to determine whether there would be any hope of recovery. The next day, Christmas, he told us that Mom suffered a massive stroke during the twenty-one minutes and that they still did not find the shunt: it must be in her heart. At noon on the 26th, he reported that the stroke was much worse than they had thought. At that point, seventy-two hours after her coronary collapse, we ordered the vent to be removed.

Now she would begin breathing on her own—she was free, her mouth was open. We resumed our prayers, comforting words, and blessings. We encouraged her to see Jesus welcoming her, to see Dad, Bob, and Megan, and to see the light, knowing that all would be well. Individually we took turns to speak with her privately; inevitably I could only keep telling her how grateful I was for her.

We did this for another seventy-two hours, right around the clock, constantly keeping vigil, watching this woman who gave us life ebb out of her own.

She died with a whisper of a breath at 10:08 on the 29th.

Is there anything like this?

Bringing someone into life is extraordinary; we encounter a new not yet known person, filled with promise. But this is so different. Here was the person who knew us best, who brought us into the world, someone who had shaped our hearts and minds and souls. We knew so much about her and she about us. This woman had loved us, and we could not but identify ourselves with her.

As many of you know who have also been through such a vigil, this *nunc dimittis* experience makes everything else in life pale by comparison. Here our moral lives are finally shaped by love and death and the promise of everything we hope for. And, if gratitude is not the operative virtue, it is hard to think what else could be.

Chapter Twenty-One

CHALLENGING WORDS

"You are going to do a doctorate."

The first set of challenging words are part of a story I told earlier about the provincial team of New York informing me that I was to do doctoral studies. I return to it because I'd like to take the story into a different context, one shaped by the two other accounts in this chapter.

In the spring of 1981, a year before my ordination to the priesthood, while studying at Weston Jesuit School of Theology, the assistant to the New York Jesuit provincial made an unannounced visit to inform me that I was to do a doctorate.

I had two immediate questions. Having been a Jesuit for eleven years, I was surprised that this decision had never been communicated to me; in fact, I thought I would be working in one of our parishes. Thus, I asked, "When did you make the decision?"

"Yesterday, at the provincial consultation. We thought you should be the first to know."

Then I turned to the second question, "A doctorate in what?"

"In urban studies or a political science. We know how good you are in community organizing and activism, but we want you to be an intellectual activist!"

I responded, "You can't afford the psychiatric bills for me to work in either of those fields."

"Well, you are going to do a doctorate. Let me know tomorrow in what other field you propose to study."

I returned to my community and told them about the very peculiar encounter. After being convinced that at least I would do well in moral theology, I saw the assistant provincial the next day. "So, what will you study?"

"Moral theology."

"Good. So where will you study?"

"OK, already!" I answered with exasperation, "I need to ask around."

At the end of a year of searching and reflecting, I followed the advice of many to study in Rome's Gregorian University with Josef Fuchs, a man whose writings I most admired and who was the senior moral theologian in the Jesuit order. I arrived in Rome in September 1982 to earn a licentiate and a doctorate; after five years I received each degree.

"YOUR BROTHER BOB DIED THIS MORNING."

Two years before I left for Rome, my twenty-six year old brother Bob suffocated during an epileptic seizure. Indeed, the words notifying me of his death will never leave my ears. Bob was 360 days younger than I. We were very close.

I had just returned to Murray-Weigel Hall at Fordham University, where I had done my undergraduate studies. I arrived the night before for a ten-day vacation in New York City. That morning I went for a jog around Edward's Parade. I felt great. A vacation was under way.

When I returned to Murray-Weigel, the receptionist told me that the rector was looking for me. All sweaty, I went in my jogging shorts and T-shirt to his office. After asking me if my brother Bob was having any difficulty, he told me that my dad had called to tell him to contact me and let me know that Bobby was just found dead.

Bob was a baker at an enormous supermarket and went to work before dawn. This morning, June 2, 1980, he got up to wash his hair.

He leaned over the tub and put his head under the faucet. At that moment he went into a seizure, and stuck between the tub and the faucet, he died of suffocation.

The day before was my niece Megan's baptism. The first born of her generation, the celebration was simply wonderful. Bob had made the cake for this occasion, a cake I can still taste.

When I called my dad he was sobbing uncontrollably, saying, "How can I tell your mother?" Eventually he would have to go to her office and tell her the news. She told me later, she looked up and saw Dad walking toward her. Oh, he's come to take me to lunch, she thought, but in seconds she saw he was distraught.

Two years later, we were all still grieving Bob's sudden death. I had been ordained in June and was setting off for studies in Rome. My mom, especially, saw my departure as painful. As I left, she and my dad asked that I be available every Friday at 12:45 when they would telephone me. For the entire first year, in each of those phone calls, my dad would speak to me and occasionally one of my siblings, but never my mom.

That first year was overwhelming. I had seven classes the first semester, all in Italian; I barely understood a word. I knew no one in my community of 120 Jesuits. I was still grieving my brother's death, alienated from my family, and second-guessing my entire decision. Besides, I was a newly ordained priest in a city where there was no shortage of priests; instead, there was a shortage of opportunity to serve.

Every Friday evening I would go to the beautiful Piazza del Campidoglio, where the bronze statue of Marcus Aurelius dominates the center, and the statue of Roma seated at the base of the Roman Senate is flanked by the gods of cornucopia. I would sit next to one of the gods with their baskets of plenty and watch tourists, especially lovers, come to see this enchanting piazza constructed by Michelangelo.

Inevitably I would start crying, for about an hour. In seminary everyone says that your first year as a priest is your happiest; mine was to date my worst. After my cry, I would return home. Fridays were tough.

In time, I became a very different person. I remained resolute in my decision, hard as it was. I made friends, accepted invitations to different communities, and cultivated my relationship with Fuchs and his colleagues. By the end of the year, one of my papers was published in a German journal, a German newspaper profiled me as a new voice, and I was establishing myself in my field, with the help of my mentor. When I returned to the New York area for a month in June 1983, my mom and dad became reconciled with my stay in Europe, and in the following fall they visited me for the first time.

"YOUR MELANOMA HAS RETURNED."

Last summer on August 6, 2008, as I was tarrying in Europe having just met with the Planning Committee for the 2010 conference in Trent, I found a lump just below my waist. It was a swollen lymph node almost four centimeters long. Having had a very thin melanoma removed from my back in November 2006, I called my primary care physician for an appointment and saw him when I returned two days later.

I was going to be in the States only five days, heading out to a conference in Manila where twenty-five moral theologians from all over East Asia would be meeting for the first time in their history. I had been asked to chair the meeting and to deliver the keynote.

My physician could find no other swollen node, and my blood showed no infection. He set me up to meet a surgeon who would remove the node when I returned from the Manila meeting. I met the surgeon on August 11th, a day before flying (thirty hours of travel!) to Manila. "I'm afraid it's your melanoma," he said. "It's near the site of your first encounter with melanoma. I want to do an emergency CAT scan to see if there are other swollen nodes." Five hours later, the report showed no other swelling. "You are returning the 23rd. You'll have surgery on the 26th. I'll excise the node and biopsy it." "OK."

My doctors told me that delaying surgery by ten days would have no impact on my health. Since I was recruited to chair this meeting in which much was invested, I was honoring an important commitment. In hindsight, I learned that by not acting on my fear, I had become stronger.

Still, as I flew to Manila, I found myself sobbing. Flying those thirty hours were probably the most destabilizing hours of my life, but I became convinced that if I did have cancer, I needed to take it in stride and to trust in God that everything would eventually work out.

I had been to Manila on four previous occasions, always to teach at the Ateneo. This time was different. I remember sitting in a cab at an intersection on Katipunan Avenue wondering whether I had cancer. Sitting alone in that cab, I was pretty anxious, but I looked out the window and saw teems of Filipinos there at that intersection. A full twelve-hour time difference from Boston, I was alone in a cab on the exact other side of the world, and Katipunan was no Commonwealth Avenue. I was literally and figuratively at the furthest point I could possibly be from my home, friends, and family. And I was wondering, do I have cancer?

That's when I saw the beggar children, the shirtless workers, and the women carrying their children. Seeing them, I realized how vulnerable life is, how fragile the wall between life and death is for hundreds of millions of people, how transient good fortune, good health, and the good life can be. I wondered how the beggar children lived and how long they would live. I wondered about the mothers' grief and the exhaustion of the workers, who realized they would never, ever have a decent wage and that their families would always be in destitute poverty. Wondering whether I had cancer, I found myself thinking of all these people whose own health and well-being was easily as precarious as my own. They lived in impasse; I was experiencing it. The worker knows there is no way out, the mother has no relief of her concerns for her children, and the beggar children will never get beyond their situation.

For the first time in my life I felt that I was not living my life by my expectations. My life was at a crossroads, and I would have to live with far less certitude, stability, and confidence. Yet, at that traffic intersection, the horizon of my life expanded enormously. I thought,

I am not alone. I have friends and family certainly, but on the other side of the world, I belonged where I was. I began to enjoy the present and the unfamiliar with far greater ease than ever before.

For the next five days in Manila, I gave lectures around the city at different hospitals and universities. Throughout, I kept seeing poor and working class people on the streets of Manila. I saw in their faces and in the pace of their walking something about the frailty of human life. It was overwhelming. Somehow instead of wondering how I would do, I saw with a new freshness how they were living, with an enormous range of challenges and infirmities. In an odd way, given my own unstable situation, I felt the immediacy of their lives where stability is a rare commodity. In that vulnerable sea of humanity, I fell into a momentary peace about my future.

On August 28th the surgeon told me, "Your melanoma has returned. You have a stage three melanoma." On September 26th, I would have major surgery to remove the lymph nodes in my left thigh. I would begin interferon infusions for one month in mid-November. Then for eleven months, I would inject myself three times a week with interferon, maintaining the maximum dosage.

Unlike those in Manila, I am treated at a major heath facility in Boston.

The news, of course, was daunting. My family, friends, colleagues, and students were as surprised as I was because I am a person of considerable health and energy. Yet, even though the horizon looked somewhat challenging and limiting, I think I will be living into the future with a vulnerability that I first encountered when I had the original melanoma removed and waited for the results. Now I will be living like that for years to come, in a more "real" time, when everything becomes present because I am surrounded by loving people, from family and friends to nurses and doctors. As frightened as I am, I know I am in their hands and that I will be fine.

Challenging words make a great deal of difference, but they come in very different ways. Some words, like the news of my brother's death, leave us breathless. There's nothing to be done; the news comes too late. The words are numbing as they echo down the years about an unalterable moment that transfixed all of us who heard them. They are words that simply leave us to pick up the pieces as we await the comfort of the resurrection.

Other challenging words do not leave us bereft and powerless. Like my call to studies, they can energize us and allow us to pursue a course of action we never anticipated. The challenge from beyond allows us to realize that, at times, anything is possible. The willingness to hear those words is key, and therein opportunity rewards the vigilant. So for me, before 1981, I never thought that I would become a moral theologian. Now I cannot imagine my life otherwise.

But these new challenging words that I heard last year are at once overwhelming and, strangely enough, manageable. For me, there's no race against time. The words are destabilizing and I wish they were never uttered, but they were, and so I find my life being changed again remarkably. While I never thought this would be, I await my future as a challenge not unlike that first year in Rome when everything was so strange and new and my anxiety at times got the best of me. Like then, this challenge, inevitably, has to be accepted.

And, like so many other people, who hear such similar words in better or worse contexts, like them and with them, I stand and wait.

Chapter Twenty-Two

WORDS OF LIFE

For several decades, there has been a growing consciousness of the need to protect human life. Certainly the human carnage in Europe and Asia during World War II is enough to jolt humanity into an awareness of the need to appreciate a clear and firm and universal support for human life.

We normally defend life through the phrase "sanctity of life." In fact, it is difficult to think of another phrase more commonly associated with contemporary Catholic moral teaching than "sanctity of life." Surprisingly, the term itself is rather new: No Catholic dictionary or encyclopedia before 1978 had an entry on it. For instance, in the fifteen-volume *New Catholic Encyclopedia of 1967*, the term has no entry. (It later appeared as a modest afterthought in an unsigned entry in the later supplement.) There is no entry in the new theological dictionaries from the United States, England, or Germany, and there is only a passing reference in an Italian counterpart.

"Sanctity of life" certainly has its roots in modern Christian writings, most commonly in the assertion of God's dominion over human life. In 1908, the Jesuit moralist Thomas Slater discussed suicide and declared, "The reason why suicide is unlawful is because we have not the free disposal of our own lives. God is the author of life and death, and He has reserved the ownership of human life to Himself."

At its roots, this prohibition against killing is about *God's* ownership: we do not own our lives; God does. Therefore, we are not free to dispose of them. In a manner of speaking human life belongs to God.

The phrase "sanctity of life" first explicitly appeared in papal writings in the encyclical *Mater et Magistra*. Still, in its original form, "sanctity of life" functioned as a euphemism for God's dominion. Thus, life is sacred because its owner, God, willed it so; like other objects that God owns and sanctifies—the marriage bond and the temple, for example—life cannot be violated. The sacredness rests not in anything intrinsic to the marriage bond, the temple, or human life; it rests on the claim of God, who made and owns the sacral quality of the marital bonds, temples, and human lives.

Pope John Paul II significantly developed the term by recognizing the sanctity of life as intrinsic to the human person. In 1987, he wrote about the inviolable right to life, saying, "The inviolability of the person, which is a reflection of the absolute inviolability of God, finds its primary and fundamental expression in the inviolability of human life."

Later, then, Cardinal Joseph Ratzinger wove these two trends into the tradition. In *Donum vitae*, he wrote:

From the moment of conception, the life of every human being is to be respected in an absolute way because man is the only creature on earth that God has 'wished for himself' and the spiritual soul of each man is 'immediately created by God'; his whole image bears the image of the Creator."

The document continues:

Human life is sacred because from its beginning it involves the 'creative action of God' and it remains forever in a special relationship with the Creator, who is its sole end. God alone is

Lord of life from its beginning until its end: no one can, under any circumstance, claim for himself the right directly to destroy an innocent human being.

This latter section is repeated later in paragraph 53 of *Evangelium Vitae* and became the single text in the *Catechism of the Catholic Church* (paragraph 2258) to interpret the Fifth Commandment. The entire paragraph was John Paul II's most extensive statement, before *Evangelium Vitae* itself, on both the sanctity of life and God as Lord of life. In it we see some of the key elements that later appear in the encyclical: that human life is singular; that we are created in God's image; that we are uniquely created by God for a special relationship with God, which is, in turn, our destiny; that God has created within us our soul which makes our lives sacred; and that, finally as source and end of human life, God is Lord of life. While not at all abandoning the "God's ownership or dominion" argument, the pope gave it newer meaning by highlighting the uniqueness of the human subject in God's image.

The act of creation is where God invests each human life with its inviolable character that now lies *within* the human, the image of God. The human is not to be killed, therefore, because of who the human is. Human life is not simply an object that God owns: human life is a subject bearing the inviolable image of God. In John Paul II's personalist writings, all people were invited to see within human life an indelible mark of its sacredness. The pope breathed life into the concept of "sanctity of life."

Because of this new foundation in teaching on life issues, the pope needed to revisit certain long-held moral norms. For instance, previously, the church permitted capital punishment. Before the encyclical, *The Catechism*, published by the Pope's own administration, had stated the traditional teaching of the church, which permitted capital punishment. But in 1997, the *Catechism* was edited and now teaches that only in the rarest instance is the death penalty morally valid and that those cases in which the execution of the offender is an absolute necessity "are very rare, if not practically non-existent" (2267).

The teaching on capital punishment has now evolved toward its abolition because now we talk about the intrinsic dignity of all people, the innocent and the guilty, through the language of sanctity of life. We act differently in part because a fundamental concept illuminated better our understanding of responsible governance.

CONSISTENT ETHICS OF LIFE

The moral relevance of "sanctity of life" was made more morally compelling by another new fundamental concept. In December 1983, Cardinal Joseph Bernardin launched an argument for a consistent life ethics. While sanctity of life would help us to appreciate the dignity of the human being as being intrinsically in the image of God, the Bernardin concept would prompt us to consider and apply the sanctity of life argument to every stage and every area of life. It would certainly compound the urgency of changing the teaching on capital punishment, but it would also bring sanctity of life to other ethical issues that were not previously considered under that rubric, issues like health care, education, and employment.

From 1983 to 1996, the cardinal gave thirty-five lectures and speeches on the topic. In these lectures he continuously extended and deepened the language of sanctity of life by applying it to abortion, euthanasia, capital punishment, standards of living, old age, disabilities, economic and social development, etc.

Together Pope John Paul II, Cardinal Ratzinger, and Cardinal Bernardin made the language of life universal, pervasive, theologically rich, and ethically relevant and urgent. With two phrases about life, bishops, priests, and laity have been able to find a way of having a unified argument and a common language about the moral need and obligation to say more about the multitudinous ways human life needs to be upheld.

Not surprisingly the language of human rights enters into the language of sanctity of life. Some may think the language of rights is inimical to Christianity, but actually it was the church who enunciated in their earliest (twelfth century) canons a recognition that for a bishop to govern, he needed rights. In time, rights language, rather than being highly individualistic as some have claimed, was fundamentally social. The common good needs that the rights of their members are upheld. Rights became the language of the church's law.

In his new encyclical, *Caritas in veritate*, Pope Benedict XVI develops and applies rights language as an extension of the fundamental right to life. Here he defends the right to food and water as integral to the right to life.

> The right to food, like the right to water, has an important place within the pursuit of other rights, beginning with the fundamental right to life. It is therefore necessary to cultivate a public conscience that considers *food and access to water as universal rights of all human beings, without distinction or discrimination.*

We can see here how the language of rights, life, and consistency come together.

LIFE-AFFIRMING ORDINARY DISCOURSE

Quite apart from the important social, legal, and civil functions that these terms have, I think that another context for promoting the language of life is by the quality of our own way of talking with others. Life-affirming discourse needs to embody a respect for humanity. Yet, many times our words do not uphold life, but rather endanger life by promoting a socially poisonous atmosphere riddled with bias, division, condescension, and a host of other negative stances. In short, words that are used to belittle another are at odds with the language of life.

We know how ethnic- and race-related jokes and comments are clear indications that some people are fundamentally intolerant of the equality and dignity of other persons. Moreover, when they act on these beliefs by making remarks of ridicule, they believe that their listeners share in their insights and implicitly validate their claims. They presume that they are safe to utter the words and that this circle of peers shares their own basic stance toward the people being mocked and derided. We have seen time and again that whenever someone within a group of people believes that they enjoy the license to talk unethically about others, they indulge themselves even more.

Here then the challenge is not only the speaker but also the listeners; listeners implicitly empower the bigot, racist, sexist, or homophobe to make comments that undermine the dignity of others. The acceptance of such remarks by a grin, a laugh, a nod, or some other expression of affirmation is nothing less than an act of acquiescence.

The so-called "innocent joke" often is not innocent. Rather, it is the indicative tip of the iceberg that reveals just how deep and pervasive is the belief in the inequality of another. In order to promote a language of life we need to be vigilant that our language upholds the dignity and sanctity of each person.

Our everyday ordinary language is just as effective in promoting human dignity as are the phrases articulated by church leaders. Putting that language into use marks a social stance in which the stranger can see that their right to life is not different from any other human being's.

Chapter Twenty-Three

WORDS OF
GREETING AND FAREWELL

I have always loved the greetings with which St. Paul begins his epistles. In Romans he concludes the beautiful greeting with these words: "To all the beloved of God in Rome, called to be holy. Grace to you and peace from God our Father and the Lord Jesus Christ. First, I give thanks to my God through Jesus Christ for all of you, because your faith is heralded throughout the world."

Then there's the magnificent greeting in First Corinthians:

> To the church of God that is in Corinth, to you who have been sanctified in Christ Jesus, called to be holy, with all those everywhere who call upon the name of our Lord Jesus Christ, their Lord and ours.
> Grace to you and peace from God our Father and the Lord Jesus Christ.

Paul extends this greeting by another four verses, assuring his readers that God will be endlessly faithful. Still, what I love about this greeting is that there is not an inkling of Paul's (later) admonition for the fractiousness of the community at Corinth. As in his greeting to the Romans, he simply addresses the church in the bounty of blessings from the Lord.

Paul's greetings are clearly a model for everyone. Rather than cutting to the chase, Paul spends time helping the recipients to be mindful of God and Jesus Christ and of their own righteousness. Every epistle begins with these lovely lush blessings.

In ordinary life we try to act similarly. Regardless of what we want to say, hear, borrow, or ask from another, we greet them first. Greeting is an initiative to reestablish a familiarity between one another. It is not simply a formality; rather, it is a sign of respect for another. We usually do not go into a conversation with another until we have greeted them.

Unfortunately, not everyone appreciates the significance of the greeting. In an uproarious essay from 1750, Samuel Johnson in *The Rambler* wrote about screech owls. Remarking about the tendency to distinguish human beings by the names of animals that a person resembles, Johnson began talking about screech owls. He writes:

These screech-owls seem to be settled in an opinion that the great business of life is to complain, and that they were born for no other purpose than to disturb the happiness of others, to lessen the little comforts, and shorten the short pleasures of our condition, by painful remembrances of the past, or melancholy prognosticks of the future; their only care is to crush the rising hope, to damp the kindling transport, and allay the golden hours of gaiety with the hateful dross of grief and suspicion.

Johnson notes that these people pounce on others who are unprepared. There is no greeting, but just the dark complaint or pessimistic claim: screech owls appear on the scene without any warning and spontaneously offer their negative prognostications. But one thing that particularly irks Johnson is not simply the pathetic comments by the screech owl, but the effect that their words have on their own selves. While they diminish the hope, joy, trust, and rightful expectations of others, they seem immune to the negativity of the very suggestions that they make. Johnson writes:

> What always raises my resentment and indignation, I do not perceive that his mournful meditations have much effect upon himself. He talks and has long talked of calamities, without discovering otherwise than by the tone of his voice that he feels any of the evils which he bewails or threatens, but has the same habit of uttering lamentations, as others of telling stories, and falls into expressions of condolence for past, or apprehension of future mischiefs, as all men studious of their ease have recourse to those subjects upon which they can most fluently or copiously discourse.

Just as their greeting is lacking, so their mindfulness of the other is omitted as well.

I do not know where you have met screech owls, but I remember them showing up for exams. Even when I was in grade school, before the teacher would come in with the exams, a screech owl would cross the threshold and without any greeting or salutation ask "who knows. . . ." His questions were always frightening: no one knew the answer because the question was so remote that it was not among our study materials. But he asked the question to jolt us. Before he entered the room, there was confidence; but this screech owl knew exactly how to depress and confuse his fellow students, and of course, he really didn't care what the answer was. After causing chaos by tapping into other's anxieties, he would go to his seat acting as if nothing had transpired.

Later on as a student at the Gregorian University, I had constant run-ins with screech owls. We had oral exams for nearly every course. Our "time" was posted always in alphabetical order, so for most of my two years of courses, I was near the same students and, unfortunately, the same screech owl. With some classes having thirty to fifty students, there could be a line of students waiting outside a professor's door, and this screech owl would arrive, sans salutation, and ask aloud the entire group of students an esoteric question that had no bearing on the material for which we were being examined. Anticipating the anxious state of his fellow students, he "greeted" us with his absurd concern. The other students became easily rattled and convinced that they were not properly prepared. This student would return to his own notes and continue studying, unfazed by the question he had just asked. Of course, he did this routinely, such are the habits of screech owls.

The key attribute that I find for the contemporary screech owl is to unsettle, which he did as soon as he arrived on the scene. But a greeting exists to settle us: we greet another to assure them that we come to see them in good faith. Thus while a greeting is precisely a settling action, the screech owl's trademark manner of asking his question was hardly a greeting. More than anything, it was a disturbing false alarm.

The way we greet one another is rather important. It is a social formula that reflects and communicates the respect we have for the colleague with whom we are initiating a conversation. Regardless of the brevity of that discourse, some greeting, "Hi, how are you?," "Good to see you," "Good morning" is called for before the conversation gets under way.

Words of Farewell

Just as our greetings assure our colleagues that we intend to engage them respectfully, so too our words of farewell have their assurances. At the end of a meeting, a conversation, or an encounter, we rarely offer any farewell that is final. We do not take our leave without assuring the other of our hope to meet again. We conclude, saying something like, "See you soon," "Until the next time," etc. The main phrases in German, Italian, and French each insist that we will be meeting again: "Auf wiedersehen," "A la prossima volta," "Au revoir."

These are not words of good-bye but rather well-wishing words for the other until we see one another again.

The liturgy has the same format. It begins with a greeting built on our triune faith: "May the grace of Our Lord Jesus Christ, the Love of God and fellowship of the Holy Spirit be with you." It ends with a blessing. The greeting and the farewell are both based on graciousness.

During my years as a doctoral student in Rome, I occasionally went to Mass at the Church of San Andrea del Valle. This enormous church is one of Rome's first baroque churches and was the setting for the first act of *Tosca*. There, too, every evening was a liturgy, the last of the day in all of central Rome. Often the priest celebrating the mass was the same. His farewell at every Mass was the same, though always memorable.

To a congregation of about twenty, after Communion and before the final blessing, he would say in a familiar way, "You are going to your homes and I to mine, you are going to your supper and I to mine. But before I go, I have one more thing to say to you." He would pause and we, in great expectation, would await his words knowing exactly what he would say, because he concluded the liturgy with these words every evening. We waited, savoring the words that he eventually uttered, the very words we longed to hear, "The Lord be with you."

Greetings and farewells are keys to good relationships. They are markers of goodwill and well-wishing. They are based on simple, familiar, frequently used, oft-repeated words. Their use allows us to see that we take no meeting for granted and that our coming, like our going, is in the context of respect.

Part V

FAITH, HOPE, AND CHARITY

Chapter Twenty-Four

THE LANGUAGE OF FAITH

Earlier I told you the story of my parents' home being destroyed in a fire. Here I return to the story to finish the telling of it, which was tragically the early and untimely death of my dad.

As you may recall, in 1990 my parents' home was destroyed in a fire. They spent the next nine months rebuilding it, so as to sell it and move to Florida. I asked my mom, why to Florida? "Because that's what you do when you retire." My dad had had emergency heart surgery several months before the fire and so, three times a week, concerned about him and her, I would drive from Fordham University to Kings Park, Long Island.

For the nine months of rebuilding, they lived in a motel where they left each morning to supervise the rebuilding and to await the move to Florida. I drove from Fordham to their hotel just to give them some support.

Everything they owned had been destroyed in the fire and, when they got to Florida, they intended to buy furniture and rebuild their own lives. Often my dad, who turned sixty-two during this time, worked at a very hard pace. On occasion I would suggest that he work with less intensity and stress. "I want to get down to Florida and hold your mother's hand while sitting on the beach. I'm tired of waiting."

They eventually sold their rebuilt house and headed to Florida. They found a condo that was still to be built. It would be ready in six months for occupancy. Thus, they lived in a rental unit and waited. In the meantime, I had joined the Weston Jesuit faculty in Cambridge, Massachusetts, and was now ninety minutes from my sister Deb, who lived in New Hampshire with her husband and two children, Megan and Jon. My sister Jean had married a few months before the fire and after my parents moved to Florida, she and her husband had bought a new home on Long Island.

After two months in Florida, Mom and Dad decided to drive up and see how Jean and her husband had settled into their home, how I was doing at Weston Jesuit, and how their grandchildren in New Hampshire were doing. When they arrived, Mom and Dad looked like they were settling into Florida.

A month after they returned to Florida, Dad suffered a heart attack and died. My mom was devastated. Losing her husband, after all the efforts of rebuilding, she felt that she had nothing: no husband, no furniture, no keepsakes, no home, no life. Fortunately my brother Sean was there in Florida.

During this time each of us tried to help my mom find some footing. As the oldest child, I began phoning her daily as I would for the next fifteen years, and I flew down to Florida with some frequency to help her settle into her new life.

DARKNESS

After my dad's death, I found that as I was falling asleep I would ask God for some assurance that my dad was well and with God. And every night while I waited for a response, I would sense nothing but a void of darkness. This occurred every night for about seven months.

I became very confused by this experience. Above all, I felt it was a lack of faith on my part. Why was I unable to believe? Why could I not trust that dad was indeed with God?

This confusion became a deeper problem. On the one hand, as a priest, I felt I could tell no one about this experience, not even my spiritual director. How could I tell the story of my prayer and of the darkness? With such an absence of faith, I could not be much of a priest, I thought. On the other hand, I wanted to know a more important matter: not the state of my faith (I knew it was weak); I wanted to know about my dad's well-being.

After seven months, it was time to see my superior for what we call the annual manifestation, or account of conscience. He asked me how I was coping, being in a new job at Weston, losing my dad a year after the fire, and having an abiding concern for my mom. "Okay," I answered. "And your health?" "Fine." "Do you have a prayerful sense of consolation; have you experienced peace from God?" "No."

I then confessed my darkness.

"Why have you let this go so long? Why didn't you tell your spiritual director?"

"I'm a priest; I should have believed more." While I was willing to confess that I was weak in my faith, I still wanted to know something more important . . . how was my dad? Yes, my faith was weak, but where was my dad?

"Faith Is a Gift."

My superior, John Libens, responded to me by simply saying:

> Faith is a gift. It's not up to you; it's from God. You asked God for an indication about your dad. The darkness, the void was God's answer. It came from God; it was not from you. You do not have a lack of faith; you were in faith asking for help. Don't be afraid of the darkness. The eventual consolation will be a gift, but the void is too.

At that time, I recalled an experience I had had twenty years earlier in the novitiate. I was concerned then too about how inadequate my faith was. I told my novice director, and he pulled out Mark's Gospel. He opened it to the ninth chapter about the curing of the boy with epilepsy. For me, this was a very poignant pericope, inasmuch as my brother Bob suffered terrible seizures from epilepsy.

I was struck by the passage, by the way Jesus finds the crowd: on the one hand he is confounded by his disciples' inability to cure the boy; on the other, he is deeply judgmental about the lack of faith of the father. I found the text disturbing. I was particularly inclined to the father. The poor man was trying to get the disciples of Jesus to heal his son; they could not. Jesus arrives and upbraids the father. The father cannot be any less frustrated than Jesus. So when Jesus laments the absence of faith, the father insists: "I believe, help me with my disbelief."

This is a parent speaking. This is an adult who is fearless; frustrated, but not to be rejected. His son's welfare is at stake. Sure, he doesn't believe enough. Sure, Jesus is the Messiah. Sure, Jesus's disciples are not terribly effective. But for the father, the matter is not his faith; the matter is his son. He capitulates: I believe, help me with my disbelief.

He was different from me in one matter. I was ashamed of my lack of faith, but he was not. He's somewhat shameless: he does not have the introversion to be ashamed. It's his son that's on his mind.

He is not much different than the Syrophenician mother (Matthew 15:27ff).

> And behold, a Canaanite woman of that district came and called out, "Have pity on me, Lord, Son of David! My daughter is tormented by a demon."
> But he did not say a word in answer to her. His disciples came and asked him, "Send her away, for she keeps calling out after us."
> He said in reply, "I was sent only to the lost sheep of the house of Israel."
> But the woman came and did him homage, saying, "Lord, help me."

He said in reply, "It is not right to take the food of the children and throw it to the dogs."

She said, "Please, Lord, for even the dogs eat the scraps that fall from the table of their masters."

Then Jesus said to her in reply, "O woman, great is your faith! Let it be done for you as you wish." And her daughter was healed from that hour.

Parents, Children, and the Language of Faith

The texts are nearly identical, no? A child purportedly possessed, a single parent accompanying the child, beseeching a healing. How desperate and frustrated they each are, no? And how does Jesus treat them? With sympathy? Astonishingly, Jesus finds fault with each parent: the father for lack of faith; the mother for not being a Jew. They, in turn, each capitulate to the judgment, but that's because the fault is beside the point. Their children are sick. That's what counts. They fight not about their faith, but about the child; there they do not capitulate—they are, instead, resilient in asking for the healing of their children.

I know how they felt. I only cared about my dad. I could not save him, but I felt as his son that I wanted to know how he was. I already knew that my faith was inadequate, but I simply wanted something else: to know about my dad's well-being.

His well-being was my real concern and insisting on that, I learned what Jesus wanted each of us to know. Jesus's lesson for me, for the father, and for the mother was the same: SPEAK UP!

From these two Scriptural texts, along with the experience of darkness, I learned to speak up. Yes, my faith was inadequate, but Christ would help me there. I could now, not in shame but in confidence say, I believe, help me in my unbelief. Christ was training me: lean on him; insist; ask again; insist; speak as an adult would, an adult defending an ill child; a child, longing for his father. Don't hesitate to speak directly to Jesus, I learned.

Relentlessly, the weeks passed. Where's Dad, I asked. Let me know that he is well. In some rare moments, the consolation came, but often it didn't. But I knew now not to be ashamed of my faith. I knew instead to ask for what I wanted. In that lesson, I learned the language of those who believe.

THE LANGUAGE OF HOPE

Last year I presided at a wedding. The couple met as undergraduates in 2002 in Glasgow, Scotland. They were both "third-year abroad students." She was from the Boston area; he was from Melbourne, Australia. During the year they fell in love, but by April of 2003 they realized that they were going to be returning to the opposite ends of the globe. Being in love, they wanted to remain with one another, for as Thomas Aquinas teaches us, love is union. This is why those who love desire to be with one another. As union, love calls us to rest and dwell with the other. As Augustine said of his love of God, I desire to rest in you, O Lord. Since love is union, nothing is more painful for those in love than to be separated.

Since they did not want to be separated, she managed to win appointments to finish her studies in Melbourne, and then from 2004 they maintained an around-the-world romance. Fortunately, they each secured positions with international firms so as to make their being together a more than occasional reality. Yet still, in order to stay together it meant giving up a lot of other opportunities, while seizing others.

So here they were, five years later. The readings they chose were splendid. Clearly they wanted me to say something about love, virtue, and wisdom, but I asked her what she specifically wanted me to say and she simply said, "We worked so hard at this relationship." I said, "How about hope?" "Yes, hope. I want to you to speak to us about hope."

HOPE BUILDS ON LOVE

I know that the tradition, from Paul to Augustine to Thomas Aquinas, tells us that hope builds on faith and that hope brings us to love. Of course, that's true, but Thomas reminds us that the virtues work in the opposite direction as well. Hope builds on love, and faith depends on hope.

By God's love and their responses, this couple was able to exchange their vows. Having worked hard for their union, they now wanted to hope for the future. In their wedding vows, they expressed exactly what their hope was: "I take you to be my spouse. I promise to be true to you in good times and in bad, in sickness and in health. I will love you and honor you all the days of my life."

These vows, these pledges are ways of saying that each has their hope in the other. Moreover, each believes that what they hope for about the future is precisely what the other hopes for. They make these vows so that their hope may be one and the same. For all marriages are built on hope.

All families are built on hope. Every fall, we start the school year here at Boston College. The freshmen arrive with great expectations, uncertain but surely mindful that they are looking forward to their next four years. Their vision is of what lies ahead.

The parents brought them here, unloaded their bags, moved them in, said good-bye, and drove off. If love is union, they were hurting as they let go of their daughter or son. I was sitting at dinner with one couple. I had met them when their second child arrived here. Their first was my student, and he wanted me to meet his newly arrived sister and his parents. Now their third of five children was coming. The mother especially was finding it very hard to have three of her children here. There were now more in Chestnut Hill than in her home in the Dominican Republic.

University life is hard, especially for the parents. The break is fairly radical. A child who has shown up for breakfast every morning in the intimacy of a family kitchen is now elsewhere, studying at a new place, meeting new friends, and learning about the world. Often as they become more involved in university life, the students contact the parents less and less, and the void that comes of their child's absence is difficult to bear.

Still the parents hope. They hope that the union that they have had will mature and flourish. They hope that what their children look for in life will be meaningful, enriching, and ennobling. They build their hope in the future on their family love for one another. They hope that their child will be part of the flourishing of their family.

Hope as Arduous

I listen to the parents. They say things like, I hope he finds himself. I hope he doesn't get hurt. I hope she finds a good mentor. I hope that what I taught her helps her to become a better person. I hope they are happy. Parents hope. And they hope a great deal.

Parents look forward to the future in hope. The union that they nourished, sustained, and forged with each and all their children is the ground of their hope. As each child faces numerous obstacles, challenges, and opportunities, parents live in this hope. Hope characterizes the stance of a loving parent as they watch their child mature and grow. Hope becomes the source of sustenance for parents as their child becomes an adult. Hope is what sustains them in the absence of the physical union with their children.

Hope always involves the arduous, writes Thomas in the *Summa Theologiae*. It is the nature of hope to be with us as we face the future as challenging. If everything about the future was eminently sensible, easy to achieve, and completely predictable, there would be no need for hope. We would be sure of the future, confident in what it brings.

But we don't have that certainty. We only have hope. It is why parents hope; why spouses hope; why Christians hope. It is also why hope is a gift from God. God knows how hard it is for us as we face our futures, so God gives us hope.

Paul, in the eighth chapter of Romans, tells us that we live in hope and that God through the Holy Spirit enters into us to help us articulate what it is that we hope for. As we pray, we pray in hope. In fact, prayer is the language of hope. The prayers of parents, the vows of spouses, this is the language of hope.

PRAYER AS THE LANGUAGE OF HOPE

I am learning more and more about the experience of prayer. I find that whenever I visit a church I see the same dynamics. I see people on their knees or seated before Christ on the cross, near the tabernacle, or by a statue of Mary, Saint Anthony, or Saint Theresa. They go asking for an answer to their prayers about the well-being of themselves or their child, spouse, neighbor, or friend. But then they stay awhile.

Christians come to church to pray, they sit or kneel or stand and make their requests and pray a Hail Mary, or some other prayer of devotion, but then they stay, they rest, they remain.

God welcomes us in our need. God knows that we need God's help. We go to God or to Mary or to a saint, but as we begin asking for our prayers to be heard, we in turn find ourselves beginning to rest for a moment. We find ourselves having prayed, and now we find ourselves being invited into a union with Christ, or the Virgin, or a saint.

In prayer we make requests, but then we are comforted and we rest in hope on the journey. We go to God to ask for help often for another in need, but then we sense such a welcome that we sit and stay. We don't leave immediately after prayer, we rather linger, thinking of Christ in his suffering or Mary in hers. We enter into a caring union, where we find an understanding of their suffering and of ours. There is an exchange of feeling and comfort.

For Christians, life is a journey, and as we move forward we are stressed and worried, alone and uncertain about the future, and so we stop for a moment and pray. In the prayer, as Paul tells us, the Holy Spirit helps us to utter what we want. We may not get an immediate answer to the prayer we make, but another assurance, the assurance of hope, is given to us to be confident in the future.

We find peace yet without knowledge, and this feeling of peace or consolation is our assurance of hope. It is built on love of God, on union with God.

In prayer we come with need for another, and we enter into union with God. God wants us to stay and to rest and to be assured. Therein we find hope and we learn anew what we have always known: that nothing will separate us from the love of God and because of that nothing will separate us from the love of another.

God loathes the absence, and God loathes the void. Because God is love, God is rather the guarantor that whatever separates us from one another will eventually become united again. God never fills the void or the absence or the separation (as Bonhoeffer taught us), but God gives us the assurance of hope that one day, all will be one and all will be well. This is why we pray, and this is why we hope.

Chapter Twenty-Six

THE LANGUAGE OF CHARITY

Throughout all his writings, Thomas Aquinas used the same one word to describe charity: union. I have always thought that the word is extraordinarily powerful. By charity we are in union with God. By charity we are in union with ourselves. By charity we are in union with our neighbor. Union is behind all of this charity, felt union, deeply affective union, intimate union.

Often Thomas tells us that the first act of love is to rest in the union. This too is splendid. When people fall in love, they simply want to be together. They want to rest with one another; they want to stay where they are with one another. They don't want to move, they don't want any change, they don't want to be separated. They rest in the union. When they inevitably have to separate for reasons of work or to return to their homes, they find themselves wanting be reunited again. They look forward to returning to each other. They want to be together, nothing more, nothing less. The language of love is the language of union.

This union is a real integration, a real convergence, a real making of two, one. That's why those who love hate separation. That's why a failed friendship is so sad or a failed marriage so difficult. That's why divorce is so traumatic. We hate the union falling apart.

Death between loved ones is a break in the union, an ultimate separation. Listen to a widow or widower. All they tell you is that their other half is gone. The union has been torn asunder. Not surprisingly, many feel they want to be with the spouse. Some even say things like they would rather die than be without their spouse. We hate the separation.

LOVE IS NEVER SATISFIED

When we love, we always want more. Once we open our hearts to another, once we love another, we yearn. Love is never satisfied.

In the *Confessions*, Augustine tells of his experience of being pursued by God and how once he became aware of God's love, he hungered for more. He describes how love is never satisfied:

Late have I loved you, O Beauty ever ancient, ever new, late have I loved you! You were within me, but I was outside, and it was there that I searched for you. In my unloveliness I plunged into the lovely things which you created. You were with me, but I was not with you. Created things kept me from you; yet if they had not been in you they would not have been at all. You called, you shouted, and you broke through my deafness. You flashed, you shone, and you dispelled my blindness. You breathed your fragrance on me; I drew in breath and now I pant for you. I have tasted you, now I hunger and thirst for more. You touched me, and I burned for your peace.

The nature of love is always to extend, always to expand, always to go beyond itself. Once we become lovers, we yearn to love more.

I am reminded of Karl Rahner's great insight that because God is love, God's nature would be at least Triune. If God was only two persons, God would want to love more. As love itself, God is Triune so that the Father loves the Son and the Spirit, and the Spirit loves the Father and the Son, and the Son loves the Father and the Spirit.

Rahner adds, because God is love, God wants to love more than God's self. So God created us so that God could love more than God's self. We are so that God can love us. The insight is deep within that memorable question from the *Baltimore Catechism*: "Why did God make me?" "God made me to know God, to love God and to serve God in this world, so we can be happy with God in the next." God made us so that we could rest with God in love forever.

Love always opens us up to new possibilities. Once we begin to love, we leave ourselves open to that enormous energy within ourselves, and it is never ever satisfied. This is why we look to love more, why married couples look to have children, why friends want to expand their circle of friends. The nature of love is to be open to expansion.

THE "ORDER" OF CHARITY

Augustine gives us the order of charity; that is, the order of who we are to love: we love God first, ourselves second, and our neighbor third. The order of charity is based on closeness. Augustine claims that God is closer to us than we are to ourselves. That's why we are called to love God before ourselves. I remember when I first heard that, I thought it one of the most remarkably consoling insights I had ever heard. And every time I hear it, I am delighted. There is something consoling about realizing how God deeply loves us. God is closer to us because God loves us even more than we love ourselves, and God rests more in ourselves than we rest in ourselves.

I have thought about this as I understand better and better parents' love for their children. Parents sometimes love their children more than the children love themselves. In that way, parents are closer to their children than their children are to themselves. This may explain why children at two and three years of age often push their parents away from them. They know how close their parents are, but they also know how deep the parents' love is that no matter how hard they push, parents will never go away. The ironic push of the child is filled with wisdom.

171

Augustine tells us next that we should love ourselves before we love another. Some may want to translate this in the key of the famous flight instructions, "In the event that oxygen is needed and you are seated next to a child, please first adjust your own mask, then assist the child." Likewise, others may resort to the psychological question: "If you don't love yourself, how can you love another?" But I think Augustine was thinking of this more complexly.

I think he wanted us to realize that in the love of God, we love God and ourselves and in the love for God and self, we want to love others. The experience of loving God and ourselves makes us want to love even more. If we love, we love more. It is not that the love of God and self makes the love of neighbor possible; it's that the love of God and self makes the love of neighbor necessary!

We Love Powerfully but Clumsily

My friend, John O'Malley, says that wherever two or more are gathered, there's bound to be an argument.

The reality of love is that it asks so much of us and because it does, we ask a lot of one another. When we love another, we want that sense of fulfillment that we yearn for, but it takes a life to learn, as Augustine did, that that love is never fulfilled.

This is the great problem for young married couples who think that only by loving each other completely will they be satisfied. In reality, if they love one another, they have to love others. They cannot get satisfied or fulfilled from each other. They will always expect more, and such expectations breed disappointment. Love goes out of itself, looking for more. (This is why there's nothing worse than a jealous lover!)

Love has great expectations. Because we expect so much, we love powerfully but clumsily. Jesus tells us, therefore, that we must be always willing to forgive. Always. He sets no limit; on the contrary, he makes the infinite, the unlimited, the norm: seven times seventy times. At no point do we cross a specific number of times of forgiving and say enough, I have forgiven enough.

Because we love, we must learn to be reconcilers. Paul calls us in 2 Corinthians 5 to be ambassadors of reconciliation. That's the only way we stay in love. It's the only way others can stay in love. We need to be reconciling if we want to love. To be able to reconcile is to be able to keep the promise of love.

AND YET . . .

Isn't it remarkable that for all this incredible experience, this intense energy, and this insatiable longing, we allow the entire scope of love to be caught up in the three brief words, "I love you."

Those words say it all. They carry within them not only the resting but also the promise; not only the fullness but also the hope; not only the offer but also the gift. The modesty of the words bears the depth of their meaning.

When we utter those words we unveil our hearts, our minds, and our souls. We stand before the other expecting a union never to be broken and always to last.

Index

About the Author

James F. Keenan, SJ, is the Founders Professor of Theology at Boston College. He has also taught at Fordham University and Weston Jesuit School of Theology. Father Keenan is the author of a number of books, including *Moral Wisdom: Lessons and Texts from the Catholic Tradition*, *The Works of Mercy: The Heart of Catholicism*, and with Daniel Harrington, SJ, *Jesus and Virtue Ethics: Building Bridges Between New Testament Studies and Moral Theology*. He is the editor of several award-winning books, including *Practice What You Preach: Virtues, Ethics and Power in the Lives of Pastoral Ministers and Their Congregations*, which won the Catholic Press Award for best work in pastoral theology, and *Catholic Ethicists on HIV/AIDS Prevention*, which won the best work in ethics from the Jesuit Honor Society, Alpha Sigma Nu. He has published more than three hundred essays, articles, and reviews in over twenty-five international journals.

Father Keenan was Consultant to the National Catholic Conference of Bishops for the Revision of the *Ethical and Religious Directives for Catholic Health Care Institutions* and a group leader of the U. S. Surgeon General's Task Force on Responsible Sexual Conduct. He has been on the editorial board of *Theological Studies* since 1991 and served on the board of directors of the Society of Christian Ethics. He is the chair of the international committee, Catholic Theological Ethics in the World Church, and helped host the First International

Cross-cultural Conference for Catholic Theological Ethicists in July 2006 in Padova, Italy. He has been a fellow at the Institute of Advanced Studies at the University of Edinburgh, the Center of Theological Inquiry, Princeton, and the Instituto Trentino di Cultura in Trent, Italy. He has been adjunct professor at the Gregorian University in Rome, Loyola School of Theology in Manila, and Dharmaram Vidya Kshetram in Bangalore. Father Keenan held the Tuohy Chair at John Carroll University, Cleveland and the Gasson Chair at Boston College.